Pearson Australia
(a division of Pearson Australia Group Pty Ltd)
459-471 Church Street, Level 1, Building B, Richmond, Victoria 3121
PO Box 23360, Melbourne, Victoria 8012
www.pearson.com.au

First published 2017 by Pearson Australia
2024 2023 2022 2021
10 9 8 7 6 5 4 3 2 1

Series Publisher: Tim Carruthers
Content and Learning Specialist: Aynur Bulut
Project Managers: Tamara D'Mello-Pirois, Emma-Jane McCarroll, Jennifer Boyce
Production Managers: Diane Leyman, Shahara Ahmed
Editor: Angela Tannous
Lead Editor: Daniel Hernández
Designers: Glen McClay, Nikki M Group, Anne Donald
Illustrators: Sunset Publishing Services, diacriTech, Nikki M Group
Typesetters: Nikki M Group
Rights and Permissions Editor: Justin Lim
Series Cover Design: Anne Donald
Cover Image: Shutterstock/Christopher Ursitti, p. i

Printed in Malaysia (CTP-VVP)

978 1 4886 1399 9

Pearson Australia Group Pty Ltd ABN 40 004 245 943

Contents

	Pearson Mathematics 7 chapter sections covered on Practice worksheet	Page
1 Whole numbers		
Skills/Practice 1A	1.1, 1.2	1
Skills/Practice 1B	1.3, 1.4	3
Skills/Practice 1C	1.5, 1.6	5
2 Integers		
Skills/Practice 2A	2.1	7
Skills/Practice 2B	2.2, 2.3	9
Skills/Practice 2C	2.4, 2.5	11
Skills/Practice 2D	2.6, 2.7	13
3 Fractions		
Skills/Practice 3A	3.1, 3.2	15
Skills/Practice 3B	3.3, 3.4	17
Skills/Practice 3C	3.5, 3.6, 3.7	19
4 Decimals, percentage and ratio		
Skills/Practice 4A	4.1, 4.2, 4.3	21
Skills/Practice 4B	4.4, 4.5	23
Skills/Practice 4C	4.6, 4.7, 4.8	25
Skills/Practice 4D	4.9, 4.10	27
5 Algebra		
Skills/Practice 5A	5.1, 5.2, 5.3	29
Skills/Practice 5B	5.4, 5.5, 5.6	31
Skills/Practice 5C	5.7, 5.8, 5.9	33
6 Measurement		
Skills/Practice 6A	6.1, 6.2	35
Skills/Practice 6B	6.3, 6.4	37
Skills/Practice 6C	6.5, 6.6	39
7 Linear equations		
Skills/Practice 7A	7.1, 7.2	41
Skills/Practice 7B	7.3	43
Skills/Practice 7C	7.4, 7.5	45
8 Angles and shapes		
Skills/Practice 8A	8.1, 8.2, 8.3	47
Skills/Practice 8B	8.4, 8.5	49
Skills/Practice 8C	8.6, 8.7, 8.8	51
9 Statistics and probability		
Skills/Practice 9A	9.1, 9.2	53
Skills/Practice 9B	9.3, 9.4, 9.5	55
Skills/Practice 9C	9.6, 9.7	57
10 Transformation and visualisation		
Skills/Practice 10A	10.1, 10.2, 10.3, 10.4	59
Skills/Practice 10B	10.5, 10.6, 10.7	61

Introduction

Welcome to the ***Pearson Mathematics 7 Homework Program***.

These homework program worksheets cover systematic and cumulative basic skills revision *and* lesson material from the *Pearson Mathematics 7* Student Book.

The features of the program:

- designed to be used with the *Pearson Mathematics 7* Student Book
- includes 31 double-sided worksheets, covering the entire year
- each worksheet includes a Skills side, which covers basic maths skills, as well as a Practice side, which covers material from the Student Book
- designed for easy correction as a whole class or individually
- results pages are included so students can track their own development.

Full answers for every question are available to teachers from the *Pearson Mathematics 7* eBook or the Pearson Places website.

Pearson Mathematics Homework Program

7

Skills worksheet results

Name: ....

Class: ....

Teacher: ....

Shade or tick the square if you got the answer correct.

Skills question	1A	1B	1C	2A	2B	2C	2D	Skill to learn	Moderate skill shown	Strong skill shown
1 Multiplying whole numbers to 12										
2 Dividing whole numbers to 12										
3 Multiplying and dividing by multiples of 10										
4 Multiplying and dividing larger numbers										
5 Number patterns										
6 Factors, multiples and primes										
7 Order of operations										
8 Fractions (+, −, ×, ÷)										
9 Fractions and decimals (simplifying, comparing, rounding)										
10 Percentages (simple)										
11 Decimals (+, −, ×, ÷)										
12 Powers and roots										
13 Number sentences										
14 Integers, algebra, substitutions										
15 Angles, location and geometry										
16 Statistics, probability and graphs										
17 Units and perimeter										
Total correct										

ISBN 978 1 4886 1399 9

Pearson Mathematics Homework Program 7

Skills worksheet results

Name: ....

Class: ....

Teacher: ....

Shade or tick the square if you got the answer correct.

Skills question	3A	3B	3C	4A	4B	4C	4D	Skill to learn	Moderate skill shown	Strong skill shown
1 Multiplying whole numbers to 12 and adding and subtracting integers										
2 Dividing whole numbers to 12										
3 Multiplying and dividing by multiples of 10										
4 Multiplying and dividing larger numbers										
5 Number patterns										
6 Factors, multiples and primes										
7 Order of operations (including integers)										
8 Fractions (+, −, ×, ÷)										
9 Fractions and decimals (simplifying, comparing, rounding)										
10 Percentages (simple)										
11 Decimals (+, −, ×, ÷)										
12 Powers and roots										
13 Number sentences										
14 Integers, algebra, substitutions										
15 Angles, location and geometry										
16 Statistics, probability and graphs										
17 Units, perimeter and area										
Total correct										

ISBN 978 1 4886 1399 9

7

Pearson Mathematics Homework Program

Skills worksheet results

Name:

Class:

Teacher:

Shade or tick the square if you got the answer correct.

Skills question	5A	5B	5C	6A	6B	6C	7A	7B	7C	Skill to learn	Moderate skill shown	Strong skill shown
1 Multiplying whole numbers to 12 and adding and subtracting integers												
2 Dividing whole numbers to 12												
3 Multiplying and dividing by multiples of 10												
4 Multiplying and dividing larger numbers												
5 Number patterns												
6 Factors, multiples and primes												
7 Integer operations												
8 Fractions (+, −, ×, ÷)												
9 Fractions and decimals (simplifying, comparing, rounding)												
10 Percentages												
11 Decimals (+, −, ×, ÷)												
12 Powers and roots												
13 Number sentences												
14 Algebra—substitution												
15 Angles, location and geometry												
16 Statistics, probability and graphs												
17 Area, volume and time												
Total correct												

ISBN 978 1 4886 1399 9

Pearson Mathematics Homework Program

7

Skills worksheet results

Name: ....

Class: ....

Teacher: ....

Shade or tick the square if you got the answer correct.

Skills question	8A	8B	8C	9A	9B	9C	10A	10B	Skill to learn	Moderate skill shown	Strong skill shown
1 Multiplying whole numbers to 12 and adding and subtracting integers											
2 Dividing whole numbers to 12											
3 Multiplying and dividing by multiples of 10											
4 Multiplying and dividing larger numbers											
5 Number patterns											
6 Factors, multiples and primes											
7 Integer operations											
8 Fractions (+, −, ×, ÷)											
9 Fractions and decimals (simplifying, comparing, rounding)											
10 Percentages											
11 Decimals (+, −, ×, ÷)											
12 Powers and roots											
13 Algebra—equations											
14 Algebra—substitution and like terms											
15 Angles, location and geometry											
16 Statistics, probability and graphs											
17 Area, volume and time											
Total correct											

  ISBN 978 1 4886 1399 9

Pearson Mathematics 7 Homework Program

Whole numbers

Skills 1A

Skills & Practice: Total marks /27

Name:

Class:

Teacher:

This side of this worksheet reviews number skills. The other side of this worksheet refers to *Pearson Mathematics 7* Chapter 1 'Whole numbers' sections 1.1 and 1.2.

1 Complete the table below:

	2	7	11	4	8	12	3	9	6
$\times 3$									

2 Complete the table below:

	27	12	36	15	33	21	18	24	9
$\div 3$									

3 Evaluate 150×10.

4 Evaluate 327×27.

5 What are the next three numbers in the sequence?

2, 5, 8, 11, …

6 Which of these are not factors of 4?

1, 2, 4, 8, 16

7 Evaluate $6 + 2 \times 4$.

8 Evaluate $\frac{1}{10} + \frac{3}{10}$.

9 Determine which is the bigger fraction.

$\frac{1}{2}$ or $\frac{1}{3}$

10 On a spelling test in English, Andy got 9 out of 10. What is this as a percentage?

11 Evaluate $0.9 - 0.7$.

12 Evaluate 2^2.

13 If $6 \times \triangle = 12$, find the value of $\triangle$.

14 If $\square = 2$, what is the value of the expression $4 \times \square + 3$?

15 If you are facing west and you turn 90° clockwise, in which direction are you now facing?

16 What is the probability of rolling a 2 on a standard six-sided die?

17 How many millimetres are in 25 cm?

Skills 1A mark: /17

ISBN 978 1 4886 1399 9

Pearson Mathematics 7 Homework Program

Whole numbers

Practice 1A

Show all your working

This side of this woksheet covers *Pearson Mathematics 7* Chapter 1 'Whole numbers' sections 1.1 and 1.2.

For online help, go to your *Pearson Mathematics 7* eBook.

1 Use the 'make easy numbers' strategy to calculate $2 \times 16 \times 5$.

2 Use the 'make easy numbers' strategy to calculate $57 + 128 + 43$.

3 Use the distributive law to calculate 49×4.

4 Jodie is shopping for new clothes. Use a mental strategy to calculate the total amount she spends if she buys the following items:
T-shirt, \$16; shorts, \$28; pants, \$34; shirt, \$22.

5 Write 4^3 in expanded form and then calculate the answer.

6 Write $3 \times 3 \times 3 \times 3 \times 3 \times 3$ in index form.

7 Evaluate $\sqrt{36}$.

8 Simplify $2^2 \times 2^3$.

9 A Pythagorean triple (or triad) is a group of three whole numbers with the following property: square the two smaller numbers and add them together and you get the third number squared. For example, 3, 4, 5 is a Pythagorean triple because $3^2 + 4^2 = 5^2$. What number less than 10 will make a Pythagorean triple with 12 and 13?

10 Evaluate $\sqrt[3]{27}$.

Practice 1A mark: /10

  ISBN 978 1 4886 1399 9

Pearson Mathematics Homework Program 7

Whole numbers

Skills 1B

Skills & Practice: Total marks /27

Name:

Class:

Teacher:

This side of this worksheet reviews number skills. The other side of this worksheet refers to *Pearson Mathematics 7* Chapter 1 'Whole numbers' sections 1.3 and 1.4.

1 Complete the table below:

	5	10	9	2	4	11	6	8	12
× 10									

2 Complete the table below:

	90	30	60	110	10	120	70	40	100
÷ 10									

3 Evaluate 800 ÷ 10.

4 Evaluate 105 × 12.

5 What are the next three numbers in the sequence?

1, 2, 4, 8, …

6 Which of these numbers are multiples of 6?

3, 24, 1, 96, 6

7 Evaluate 2 × 4 – 3 × 2.

8 Evaluate $\frac{3}{8} \times \frac{1}{3}$.

9 What is 0.46 rounded to 1 decimal place?

10 In a recent basketball game, Thao got 4 of her 5 shots in. What is this as a percentage?

11 Evaluate 1.2 + 2.4.

12 Evaluate 1^3.

13 If 9 – * = 4, find the value of *.

14 If ∇ = 1, what is the value of the expression 12 ÷ ∇ – 5?

15 Measure this angle using a protractor.

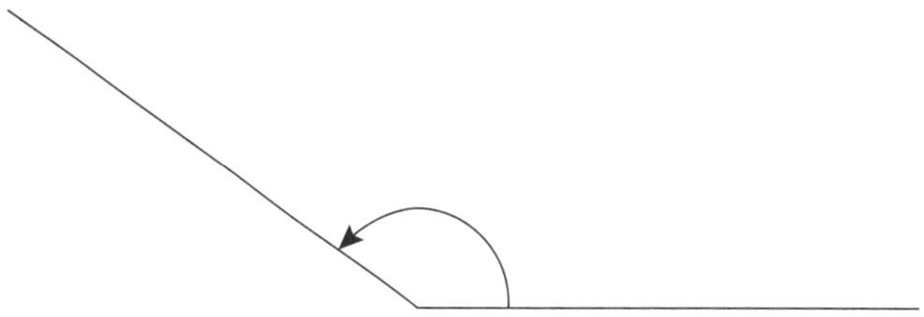

16 Decide whether you would describe the event 'I will eat lunch tomorrow' as 'impossible', 'not likely', 'likely' or 'certain'.

17 How many metres are in 3400 cm?

Skills 1B mark: /17

ISBN 978 1 4886 1399 9

Pearson Mathematics 7 Homework Program

Whole numbers

Practice 1B

Show all your working

This side of this worksheet covers *Pearson Mathematics 7* Chapter 1 'Whole numbers' sections 1.3 and 1.4.

For online help, go to your *Pearson Mathematics 7* eBook.

1 Calculate 18×6 using the 'work in stages' strategy.

2 Calculate 18×22 using an array.

3 Calculate 600×12.

4 Calculate $2700 \div 30$ using any suitable strategy.

5 You can buy tickets to the movies in bulk. If 20 tickets cost $240, how much does one ticket cost?

6 Sienna estimates that she sends 22 text messages per day. Calculate how many text messages she would send in a month with 30 days.

7 Round 449 to the first digit.

8 Estimate 52×41 by rounding to the first digit. State whether the actual answer will be higher or lower than the estimate.

9 Use rounding to the first digit to estimate an answer to $4545 \div 52$. State whether the actual answer will be higher or lower than the estimate.

10 Estimate $1363 - 947$ by first rounding each number to the nearest 10.

Practice 1B mark: /10

ISBN 978 1 4886 1399 9

Pearson Mathematics 7 Homework Program

Whole numbers

Skills 1C

Skills & Practice: Total marks /27

Name:

Class:

Teacher:

This side of this worksheet reviews number skills. The other side of this worksheet refers to *Pearson Mathematics 7* Chapter 1 'Whole numbers' sections 1.5 and 1.6.

1 Complete the table below:

	12	2	7	9	4	11	6	8	3
$\times 7$									

2 Complete the table below:

	21	56	84	35	77	49	63	28	42
$\div 7$									

3 Evaluate 562×10.

4 Evaluate 712×21.

5 What are the next three numbers in the sequence?

1, 2, 4, 7, 11, …

6 State which of these numbers are prime numbers.

2, 3, 4, 5, 6, 7, 8

7 Evaluate $12 - 5 \times 2$.

8 Evaluate $1\frac{1}{2} - \frac{1}{2}$.

9 Insert a < or > symbol to make the statement true.

$\frac{3}{4}$ ☐ $\frac{3}{5}$

10 A contestant on a television game show got 6 out of 10 questions correct. What is this as a percentage?

11 Evaluate $4.5 \div 9$.

12 Evaluate $\sqrt{16}$.

13 If $\triangle + 5 = 25$, find the value of $\triangle$.

14 If ☺ = 5, what is the value of the expression $3 \times (5 - ☺) + 1$?

15 How many sides does a pentagon have?

16 The students in a class were surveyed on their favourite type of sport.

Sport	Frequency
Netball	4
Soccer	7
AFL	8
Basketball	6
Other	1
Total	**26**

What was the second most popular sport?

17 Find the perimeter (in millimetres) of a rectangle that has width 12 mm and length 20 mm.

Skills 1C mark: /17

ISBN 978 1 4886 1399 9

Pearson Mathematics 7 Homework Program

Whole numbers

Practice 1C

This side of this worksheet covers *Pearson Mathematics 7* Chapter 1 'Whole numbers' sections 1.5 and 1.6.

For online help, go to your *Pearson Mathematics 7* eBook.

1 Evaluate $16 + 10 \div 2 - 5$.

2 Evaluate $12 + 30 \div (2 \times 5) - 10 + 3 \times 2$.

3 Insert brackets to make this statement true:

$5 + 6 \times 3 - 10 = 23$

4 Insert brackets to make this statement true:

$4 + 6 \div 3 - 1 = 7$

5 Complete the following using each of the numbers 1, 2, 4, 6 and 12 once only.

_____ + (_____ + _____) ÷ _____ − _____ = 12

6 Two numbers have a sum of 15 and a product of 54. What are the two numbers?

7 Caden completed 4.2 km of deliveries from the pharmacy straight after school. He then went to the supermarket, which was a 1.5 km trip each way. After this he went for a 5.5 km jog to train for a cross-country run. How far did he travel altogether?

8 Jackie wants to buy some seedlings. She can buy 3 for 90 cents or 6 for $1.50. Which option is better value for money?

9 Taavi is training for the school athletics carnival. How many laps of a 400 m track will Taavi need to do to jog 3.6 km altogether?

10 If Akio's dad is 179 cm tall and Akio is 141 cm tall, what is the difference in their heights?

Practice 1C mark: /10

ISBN 978 1 4886 1399 9

Pearson Mathematics 7 Homework Program

Integers

Skills 2A

Skills & Practice: Total marks /27

Name: ....

Class: ....

Teacher: ....

This side of this worksheet reviews number skills. The other side of this worksheet refers to *Pearson Mathematics 7* Chapter 2 'Integers' section 2.1.

1 Complete the table below:

	6	9	5	12	7	4	11	3	8
$\times 5$									

2 Complete the table below:

	30	5	45	35	15	40	25	55	20
$\div 5$									

3 Evaluate $67\,000 \div 10$.

4 Evaluate 569×35.

5 What are the next two numbers in the sequence?

$\frac{1}{2}, \frac{3}{4}, 1, 1\frac{1}{4}, \ldots$

6 Which of the factors of 24 are prime numbers?

7 Evaluate $1 + 3 \times 2 - 4 \div 2$.

8 Evaluate $\frac{5}{12} - \frac{1}{12}$.

9 Insert a < or > symbol to make the statement true.

$\frac{6}{7} \; \square \; \frac{7}{6}$

10 What is 20% of \$500?

11 Evaluate $0.36 \div 6$.

12 Evaluate $\sqrt{36}$.

13 If ☺ + 22 = 30, find the value of ☺.

14 If $\triangle = 3$, what is the value of the expression $4 \times \triangle - 5$?

15 If you are facing south and you turn 360° clockwise, in which direction are you now facing?

16 Halley has to hand in her Maths homework, but she has forgotten one entry. The task was to note the colour of cars in the shopping centre car park. What is the missing entry?

Car colour	Frequency
White	9
Blue	5
Red	4
Black	
Grey	6
Yellow	1
Other	13
Total	**40**

17 How many centimetres are in 1.3 m?

Skills 2A mark: /17

ISBN 978 1 4886 1399 9

Pearson Mathematics 7 Homework Program

Integers

Practice 2A

Show all your working

This side of this worksheet covers *Pearson Mathematics 7* Chapter 2 'Integers' section 2.1.

For online help, go to your *Pearson Mathematics 7* eBook.

1 Find the lowest common multiple of 6 and 8.

2 Circle the numbers that are divisible by 6.

326, 1110, 962 364, 154 111

3 Find all the factors of 36.

4 Find all the factors of 45.

5 Find all the common factors of 42 and 28 and state the highest common factor (HCF).

6 Find the HCF of 32 and 60.

7 Which of the following is not a multiple of 6?

60, 16, 66, 600, 72

8 Find the lowest number greater than 70 that is divisible by 12.

9 Mr Wu has 40 lollies to share out as prizes. He can award 20 prizes of 2 lollies each. List all the other ways he can divide the 40 lollies into equal prizes.

10 Mr Hosni's classroom currently has 25 desks arranged in 5 rows of 5 desks. One desk is never used, so he decides to move it out and rearrange the remaining desks. He wants every row to have the same number of desks. What are all the combinations of rows of desks that he could have?

Practice 2A mark: /10

ISBN 978 1 4886 1399 9

Pearson Mathematics 7 Homework Program

Integers

Skills 2B

Skills & Practice: Total marks /27

Name: ....

Class: ....

Teacher: ....

This side of this worksheet reviews number skills. The other side of this worksheet refers to *Pearson Mathematics 7* Chapter 2 'Integers' sections 2.2 and 2.3.

1 Complete the table below:

	6	3	8	10	12	7	11	9	5
× 11									

2 Complete the table below:

	132	44	99	11	55	110	33	88	121
÷ 11									

3 Evaluate 390×100.

4 Evaluate 116×77.

5 What are the next two numbers in the sequence?

288, 144, 72, 36, …

6 Is 3 a factor of 339?

7 Evaluate $(8 + 3 \times 2) \div 7$.

8 Evaluate $\frac{5}{6} - \frac{2}{6}$.

9 Which of these fractions are equal to a half?

$\frac{2}{4}, \frac{5}{9}, \frac{4}{8}, \frac{2}{3}, \frac{4}{7}$

10 Find 10% of \$250.

11 Evaluate $0.60 - 0.52$.

12 Evaluate 7^2.

13 If $\triangle \times 10 = 90$, find the value of $\triangle$.

14 If $\diamond = 4$, what is the value of the expression $\diamond \div 2 - 1$?

15 If you are facing east and you turn 180° clockwise, in which direction are you now facing?

16 What is the probability of rolling a 4 using a 10-sided die (with its faces numbered 1–10)?

17 How many kilometres are in 2400 m?

Skills 2B mark: /17

ISBN 978 1 4886 1399 9

Pearson Mathematics Homework Program 7

Integers

Practice 2B

Show all your working

This side of this worksheet covers *Pearson Mathematics 7* Chapter 2 'Integers' sections 2.2 and 2.3.

For online help, go to your *Pearson Mathematics 7* eBook.

1 What is the next prime number after 51?

2 List all the prime numbers between 5^2 and 6^2.

3 What is the next composite number after 40?

4 Are 6 and 8 co-prime? Why or why not?

5 Draw a factor tree for 36.

6 Draw a factor tree for 160, and then express the number as a product of its prime factors in index form.

7 Express 60 as a product of its prime factors in index form.

8 Find the highest common factor of 12 and 20.

9 What number is the product of the prime factorisation $2^3 \times 3 \times 5^2$?

10 24 written as a product of its prime factors is $2 \times 2 \times 2 \times 3$, and 27 written as a product of its prime factors is $3 \times 3 \times 3$. What is $648 = 24 \times 27$, written as a product of its prime factors in index form?

Practice 2B mark: /10

  ISBN 978 1 4886 1399 9

Pearson Mathematics 7 Homework Program

Integers

Skills 2C

Skills & Practice: Total marks /27

Name:

Class:

Teacher:

This side of this worksheet reviews number skills. The other side of this worksheet refers to *Pearson Mathematics 7* Chapter 2 'Integers' sections 2.4 and 2.5.

1 Complete the table below:

	6	12	3	9	4	7	2	8	5
$\times 4$									

2 Complete the table below:

	12	20	28	4	32	24	36	48	16
$\div 4$									

3 Evaluate $8100 \div 100$.

4 Evaluate 461×41.

5 What are the next three numbers in the sequence?

5, 9, 13, 17, …

6 List all the multiples of 7 between 50 and 80.

7 Evaluate $3 \times (12 - 6) \div 2$.

8 Evaluate $\frac{1}{2} \times \frac{1}{3}$.

9 What is 0.135 rounded to 2 decimal places?

10 In a recent football game, James got a goal from one of his four attempts. What is this as a percentage?

11 Evaluate $0.9 + 1.2$.

12 Evaluate 3^3.

13 If ☎ − 7 = 10, find the value of ☎.

14 If ☺ = 1, what is the value of the expression 12 ÷ (☺ + 5)?

15 Measure this angle using a protractor.

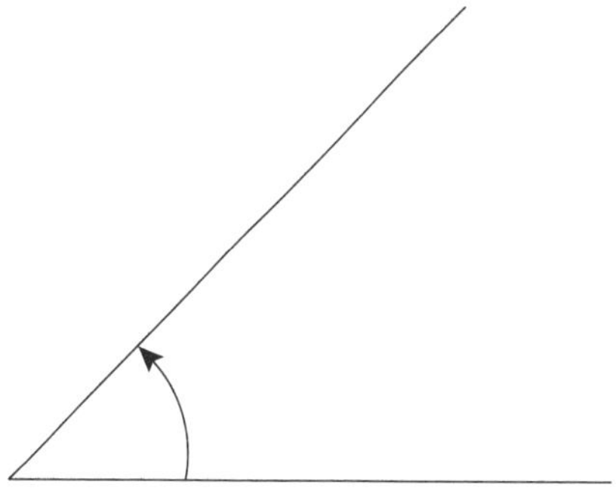

16 Decide whether you would describe the event 'I will win 1 million dollars today' as 'impossible', 'not likely', 'likely' or 'certain'.

17 How many centimetres are in 7.5 metres?

Skills 2C mark: /17

ISBN 978 1 4886 1399 9

Pearson Mathematics Homework Program 7

Integers

Practice 2C

Show all your working

This side of this worksheet covers *Pearson Mathematics 7* Chapter 2 'Integers' sections 2.4 and 2.5.

For online help, go to your *Pearson Mathematics 7* eBook.

1 Write a < or > between the numbers to make a true statement.

3 ___ -4

2 Arrange these numbers in ascending order (from smallest to largest).

-5, -3, -7, -2, 0, -6

3 Arrange these numbers in descending order (from largest to smallest).

-9, 2, 0, -3, 5, -6

4 What is the opposite of north 70 m?

5 Write the next three numbers in the sequence.

5, 2, -1, …

6 These are the minimum temperatures (in °C) in Canberra during one week in July:

-2, -5, -1, 0, -3, -4, -2.

What was the lowest temperature?

7 Use a number line to calculate the following addition.

-2 + 1

8 Use a number line to calculate the following.

7 – 8

9 Calculate 9 – 12 + 4.

10 A swimmer dives from a 5 m board and sinks 8 m under the water before rising to the surface.

Write an addition of three directed numbers to show the dive from the board, into the water and back to the surface.

Practice 2C mark: /10

ISBN 978 1 4886 1399 9

Pearson Mathematics Homework Program 7

Integers

Skills 2D

Skills & Practice: Total marks /27

Name:

Class:

Teacher:

This side of this worksheet reviews number skills. The other side of this worksheet refers to *Pearson Mathematics 7* Chapter 2 'Integers' sections 2.6 and 2.7.

1 Complete the table below:

	9	4	7	12	5	11	3	8	6
× 6									

2 Complete the table below:

	66	36	12	48	72	24	54	42	30
÷ 6									

3 Evaluate $4300 \div 10$.

4 Evaluate 694×36.

5 What are the next three numbers in the sequence?

32, 27, 22, 17, …

6 What is the next prime number after 20?

7 Evaluate $2 + 12 \div 3 + 3 \times 3$.

8 Evaluate $\frac{3}{5} + \frac{2}{5}$.

9 Insert a < or > symbol to make the statement true.

$\frac{5}{7}$ ☐ $\frac{4}{7}$

10 What is 20% of 400 g?

11 Evaluate 0.2×3.

12 Evaluate $\sqrt{64}$.

13 If ❤ ÷ 3 = 8, find the value of ❤.

14 If ☺ = 3, what is the value of the expression (5 – ☺) × 4?

15 Is this angle closer to 40 or 50 degrees?

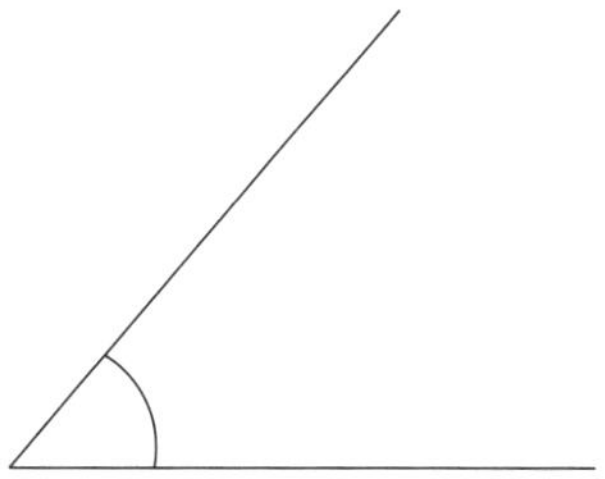

16 Police measured the speeds of 30 vehicles driving past a school. The results were put into a frequency table.

Speed (km/h)	Frequency
0–40	19
41–50	8
51–60	2
61–100	1
Total	**30**

How many vehicles were travelling above the 40 km/h speed limit?

17 Find the perimeter (in centimetres) of an equilateral triangle that has a side length of 4 cm.

Skills 2D mark: /17

ISBN 978 1 4886 1399 9

Pearson Mathematics 7 Homework Program

Integers

Practice 2D

Show all your working

This side of this worksheet covers *Pearson Mathematics 7* Chapter 2 'Integers' sections 2.6 and 2.7.

For online help, go to your *Pearson Mathematics 7* eBook.

1 Use a number line to work out the following addition.

-3 + (-1)

2 Use a number line to work out the following subtraction.

2 – (-4)

3 Use a number line to work out the following subtraction.

-4 – (-7)

4 Calculate 3 + (-2) – (-5).

5 Explain why -2 + (-5) and -2 – 5 have the same answer.

6 Work out this subtraction by simplifying first. Use a number line if it helps.

-3 – (+1)

7 Evaluate 13 + (-5).

8 Evaluate -4 + 6 – 2.

9 Fill in the missing directed numbers so that each row, column and diagonal adds to the same total.

7	-7	-6	4
-4	2	1	
	-2		
			-8

10 Evaluate 12 + (+3) – (-4).

Practice 2D mark: /10

  ISBN 978 1 4886 1399 9

Pearson Mathematics 7 Homework Program

Fractions

Skills 3A

Skills & Practice: Total marks /27

Name: ....

Class: ....

Teacher: ....

This side of this worksheet reviews number skills. The other side of this worksheet refers to *Pearson Mathematics 7* Chapter 3 'Fractions' sections 3.1 and 3.2.

1 Complete the table below:

	3	4	7	12	8	11	9	10	6
× 6									

2 Complete the table below:

	12	36	24	72	66	18	60	120	6
÷ 6									

3 Evaluate 340×100.

4 Evaluate 342×12.

5 What are the next three numbers in the sequence?

2, 5, 8, 11, …

6 Which of these is not a factor of 6?

1, 2, 3, 6, 12

7 Evaluate $1 + 2 \times 3 - 3$.

8 Evaluate $\frac{3}{7} + \frac{2}{7}$.

9 Which of these fractions is greater than a half?

$\frac{3}{8}$, $\frac{4}{10}$, $\frac{6}{11}$, $\frac{1}{6}$, $\frac{4}{9}$

10 Find 20% of $400.

11 Evaluate $0.62 - 0.51$.

12 Evaluate 3^2.

13 If $3 \times \triangle = 21$, find the value of $\triangle$.

14 If $\diamond = 9$, what is the value of the expression $2 \times \diamond - 1$?

15 If you are facing north and you turn 90° anticlockwise, in which direction are you now facing?

16 What is the probability of landing on an even number on this spinner?

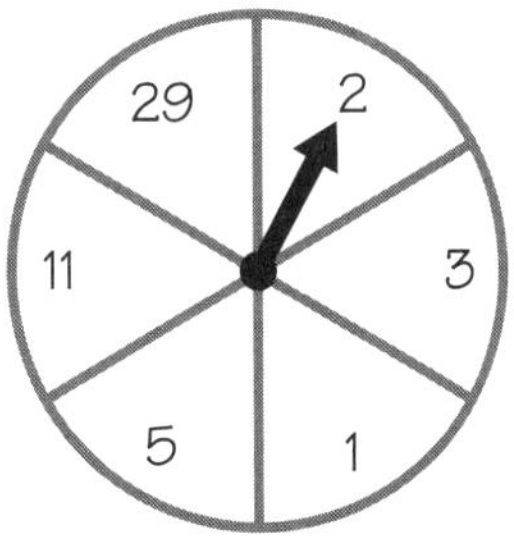

17 How many millimetres are in 4.3 cm?

Skills 3A mark: /17

ISBN 978 1 4886 1399 9

Pearson Mathematics Homework Program 7

Fractions

Practice 3A

Show all your working

This side of this worksheet covers *Pearson Mathematics 7* Chapter 3 'Fractions' sections 3.1 and 3.2.

For online help, go to your *Pearson Mathematics 7* eBook.

1 I cook a delicious batch of a dozen muffins and somebody eats $\frac{3}{4}$ of the batch. How many muffins are left? (*Note:* 1 dozen = 12)

2 What fraction of this shape is shaded?

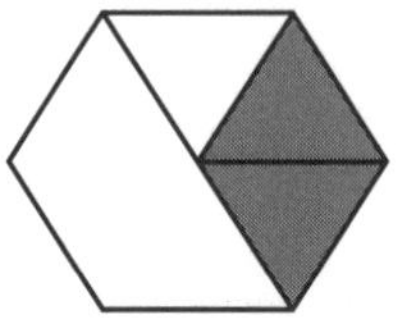

3 On the number line below, mark in these fractions: $\frac{1}{4}, \frac{5}{4}, \frac{3}{4}, -\frac{2}{4}, \frac{8}{4}$

4 What fraction of this collection of shapes is stars?

5 Complete the following to make equivalent fractions.

$\frac{50}{70} = \frac{5}{\square} = \frac{\square}{14}$

6 Write the fraction $\frac{24}{56}$ in its simplest form.

7 Siobhan was trying to simplify $\frac{120}{420}$ but didn't know the highest common factor of 120 and 420. She decided to use repeat cancelling for the factors she did know. These are her workings:

$\frac{120}{420} = \frac{12}{42} = \frac{6}{21} = \frac{2}{6} = \frac{1}{3}$

She made one mistake. Circle where the mistake was made. What should the answer have been?

8 Write $\frac{45}{7}$ as a mixed number.

9 Write $\frac{27}{6}$ as a mixed number in simplest form.

10 Write the mixed number $5\frac{7}{8}$ as an improper fraction.

Practice 3A mark: /10

  ISBN 978 1 4886 1399 9

Pearson Mathematics 7 Homework Program

Fractions

Skills 3B

Skills & Practice: Total marks /27

Name:

Class:

Teacher:

This side of this worksheet reviews number skills. The other side of this worksheet refers to *Pearson Mathematics 7* Chapter 3 ‘Fractions’ sections 3.3 and 3.4.

1 Complete the table below:

	3	4	7	12	8	11	9	10	6
× 5									

2 Complete the table below:

	10	25	60	15	20	55	75	5	50
÷ 5									

3 Evaluate $700 \div 10$.

4 Evaluate 231×23.

5 What are the next three numbers in the sequence?

1, 2, 4, 8, 16, …

6 Which of these are multiples of 8?

16, 2, 80, 4, 8

7 Evaluate $(4 + 4 \times 2) \div 3$.

8 Evaluate $\frac{3}{4} \times \frac{1}{7}$.

9 Round 0.547 to 1 decimal place.

10 I have $50 in savings. If I give 10% of this to a charity, how much have I donated?

11 Evaluate $7.23 - 5.14$.

12 Evaluate 2^3.

13 If $12 \div \square = 6$, find the value of $\square$.

14 If ☺ = 2, what is the value of the expression ☺ + ☺ + 3 × ☺?

15 What is the value of the angle *a*?

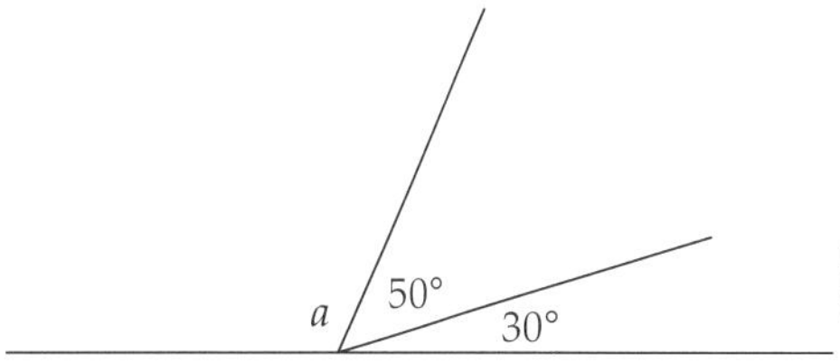

16 Three relay teams competed in a race. Which team won? How many minutes ahead of the second team were they?

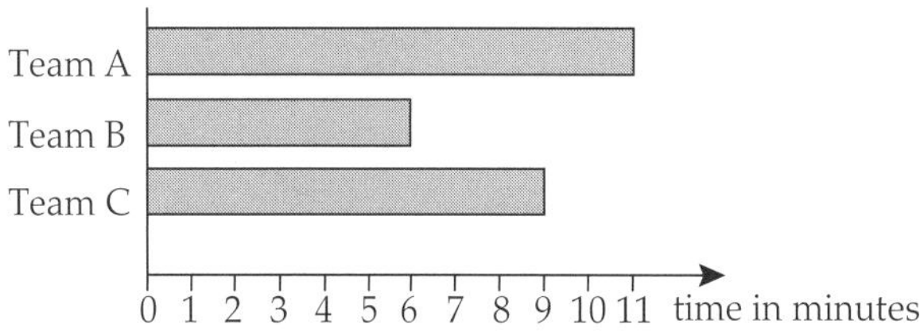

17 Find the area of this rectangle in square centimetres.

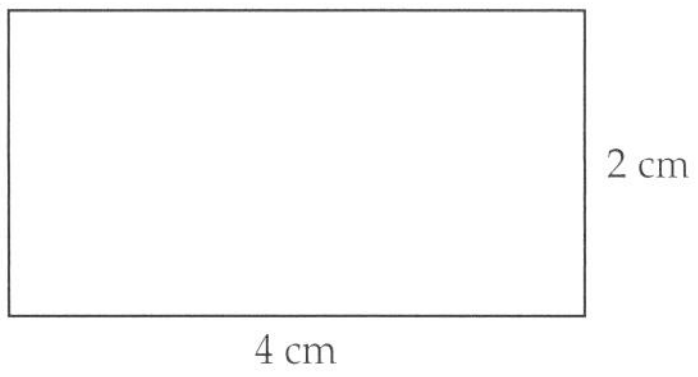

Skills 3B mark: /17

ISBN 978 1 4886 1399 9

Pearson Mathematics Homework Program 7

Fractions

Practice 3B

Show all your working

This side of this worksheet covers *Pearson Mathematics 7* Chapter 3 'Fractions' sections 3.3 and 3.4.

For online help, go to your *Pearson Mathematics 7* eBook.

1 Determine which is the larger fraction:

$\frac{3}{7}$ or $\frac{5}{11}$

2 Write this list in ascending order (from smallest to largest).

$\frac{1}{2}, -\frac{1}{3}, \frac{1}{4}, \frac{5}{6}, \frac{3}{8}$

3 Calculate the following.

$\frac{3}{7}+\frac{2}{7}$

4 Calculate the following. (Write your answer as a mixed number if appropriate.)

$\frac{7}{10}+\frac{8}{10}$

5 Calculate the following.

$\frac{12}{13}-\frac{7}{13}$

6 Calculate the following.

$\frac{8}{17}+\frac{12}{17}-\frac{3}{17}$

7 Calculate the following. (Write your answer as a mixed number if appropriate.)

$\frac{2}{3}+\frac{3}{4}$

8 Calculate the following. (Write your answer as a mixed number if appropriate.)

$\frac{8}{11}-\frac{2}{5}$

9 Calculate the following. (Write your answer as a mixed number if appropriate.)

$\frac{3}{8}+\frac{5}{6}+\frac{1}{3}$

10 Calculate the following. (Write your answer as a mixed number if appropriate.)

$4\frac{3}{4}-1\frac{7}{8}$

Practice 3B mark: /10

ISBN 978 1 4886 1399 9

Pearson Mathematics Homework Program 7

Fractions

Skills 3C

Skills & Practice: Total marks /27

Name: ....

Class: ....

Teacher: ....

This side of this worksheet reviews number skills. The other side of this worksheet refers to *Pearson Mathematics 7* Chapter 3 'Fractions' sections 3.5, 3.6 and 3.7.

1 Complete the table below:

	3	4	7	12	8	11	9	10	6
$\times 2$									

2 Complete the table below:

	120	22	12	4	6	200	20	16	64
$\div 2$									

3 Evaluate 324×1000.

4 Evaluate 124×34.

5 What are the next three numbers in the sequence?

3, 8, 14, 21, …

6 From the following, state which numbers are not prime:

1, 2, 3, 4, 5, 6, 7, 8, 9

7 Evaluate $(2 + 4 \times 3) \div 7 + 2$.

8 Calculate $\frac{7}{8} - \frac{1}{4}$.

9 Insert a < or > symbol to make the statement true.

$\frac{7}{8}$ ☐ $\frac{7}{9}$

10 What is 50% of 300 g ?

11 Evaluate $2.4 \div 8$.

12 Evaluate $\sqrt{9}$.

13 If ☆ − 3 = 10, find the value of ☆.

14 If ◇ = 3, what is the value of the expression 3 × (◇ − 2) + 6?

15 How many degrees does the little square in the triangle below represent?

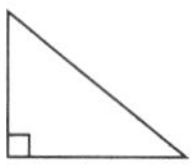

16 The students in a class surveyed what pets they each owned.

Pet	Frequency
Dog	15
Cat	9
Rat	2
Bird	1
Total	**27**

What was the most popular pet?

17 How many centimetres are in 3.4 m?

Skills 3C mark: /17

ISBN 978 1 4886 1399 9

Pearson Mathematics 7 Homework Program

Fractions

Practice 3C

Show all your working

This side of this worksheet covers *Pearson Mathematics 7* Chapter 3 'Fractions' sections 3.5, 3.6 and 3.7.

For online help, go to your *Pearson Mathematics 7* eBook.

1 Calculate the following.

$\frac{3}{23} \times \frac{5}{2}$

2 Calculate the following.

$8 \times 5\frac{3}{6}$

3 Calculate the following. (Write your answer in its simplest form.)

$\frac{3}{4}$ of $\frac{2}{9}$

4 Ibrahim earns $99 from working at Pizza Planet, and two-ninths of his income is taken in tax. How much does he have after tax?

5 Calculate the following. (Write your answer as a mixed number if appropriate.)

$\frac{2}{3}$ of $3\frac{1}{3}$

6 Calculate the following.

$12 \div \frac{8}{10}$

7 Calculate the following.

$\frac{3}{12} \div 9$

8 Calculate the following.

$1\frac{3}{7} \div 3\frac{6}{8}$

9 Sports-4-Sale is having a major stocktake sale of its running shoes and all prices are reduced by a third. How much would a pair of running shoes cost if they were originally $117?

10 Sofia promised her parents that she would complete 6 hours of homework every week. If she did 20 minutes of homework on a Monday night, what fraction of the weekly total was this?

Practice 3C mark: /10

ISBN 978 1 4886 1399 9

Pearson Mathematics 7 Homework Program

Decimals, percentage and ratio

Skills 4A

Skills & Practice: Total marks /27

Name:

Class:

Teacher:

This side of this worksheet reviews number skills. The other side of this worksheet refers to *Pearson Mathematics 7* Chapter 4 'Decimals, percentage and ratio' sections 4.1, 4.2 and 4.3.

1 Complete the table below:

	11	2	7	4	8	5	9	6	12
× 11									

2 Complete the table below:

	33	44	88	132	55	121	11	110	66
÷ 11									

3 Evaluate 54 200 × 100.

4 Evaluate 274 × 33.

5 What are the next three numbers in the sequence?

1, 1, 2, 3, 5, 8, 13, …

6 Find the lowest common multiple of 6 and 9.

7 Calculate (5 × 2 + 4) ÷ (3 + 4).

8 Calculate $\frac{1}{3} + \frac{1}{6}$.

9 Which of these fractions are equal to one quarter?

$\frac{1}{8}, \frac{2}{8}, \frac{3}{9}, \frac{3}{12}, \frac{1}{2}$

10 Find 30% of $800.

11 Find 4.6 – 1.9.

12 Evaluate 9^2.

13 If 512 × △ = 512, find the value of △.

14 If ♥ = 2, what is the value of the expression ♥ × ♥ – 1?

15 If you are facing west and you turn 90° anticlockwise, in which direction are you now facing?

16 There are 6 soccer balls, 5 basketballs and 4 volleyballs in a bag. What is the largest number of balls you could possibly take from the bag before you get a basketball?

17 How many kilometres are in 3 000 000 cm?

Skills 4A mark: /17

ISBN 978 1 4886 1399 9

Pearson Mathematics 7 Homework Program

Decimals, percentage and ratio

Practice 4A

Show all your working

This side of this worksheet covers *Pearson Mathematics 7* Chapter 4 'Decimals, percentage and ratio' sections 4.1, 4.2 and 4.3.

For online help, go to your *Pearson Mathematics 7* eBook.

1 Write $5 + \frac{3}{10} + \frac{1}{100} + \frac{2}{1000}$ as a decimal.

2 Write 18.052 in expanded word form.

3 Insert either $<$ or $>$ to make the following statement true.

0.641 59 ___ 0.641 62

4 The following results represent the throws of four different athletes in a discus event. List them in ascending order. All values are in metres.

68.51, 68.15, 68.051, 68.501

5 Round 3.8129 to 3 decimal places.

6 Round 6.512 459 to the nearest ten-thousandth.

7 Round 128.599 43 to 3 decimal places.

8 Convert 3.92 into a mixed number in simplest form.

9 Convert 7.0055 into a mixed number in simplest form.

10 Convert $\frac{4}{5}$ into a decimal.

Practice 4A mark: /10

ISBN 978 1 4886 1399 9

Pearson Mathematics 7 Homework Program

Decimals, percentage and ratio

Skills 4B

Skills & Practice: Total marks /27

Name:

Class:

Teacher:

This side of this worksheet reviews number skills. The other side of this worksheet refers to *Pearson Mathematics 7* Chapter 4 'Decimals, percentage and ratio' sections 4.4 and 4.5.

1 Complete the table below:

	9	5	7	2	12	4	8	3	6
$\times 3$									

2 Complete the table below:

	21	9	24	18	33	15	36	27	6
$\div 3$									

3 Evaluate $37\,000 \div 100$.

4 Evaluate 395×21.

5 What are the next two numbers in the sequence?

3, 6, 12, 24, …

6 Which of the following numbers are divisible by 4?
122, 132, 92, 372, 440

7 Calculate $(3 + (2 + 3) \div 5) \times 2$.

8 Calculate $\frac{2}{5} \times \frac{1}{4}$.

9 What is 19.999 rounded to 1 decimal place?

10 In a recent Maths quiz, Sam got 18 of the 20 questions correct. What is this as a percentage?

11 Find $6.5 + 5.6$.

12 Evaluate 2^3.

13 If ☎ − 7 = 11, find the value of ☎.

14 If ☺ = 7, what is the value of the expression 3 × 5 − ☺ × 2?

15 Measure this angle using a protractor.

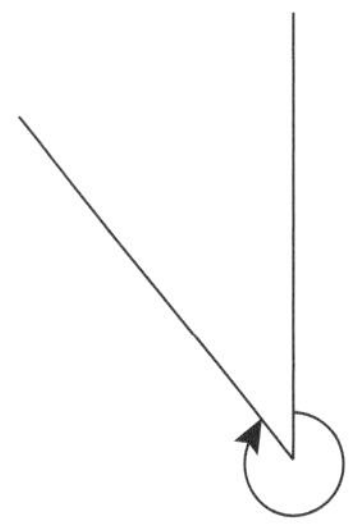

16 On her last three Science homework sheets, Mara got marks of 24, 20 and 22. What is her average mark for these sheets?

17 What is the area (in cm^2) of a carpet square that has a side length of 40 cm?

Skills 4B mark: /17

ISBN 978 1 4886 1399 9

Pearson Mathematics 7 Homework Program

Decimals, percentage and ratio

Practice 4B

Show all your working

This side of this worksheet covers *Pearson Mathematics 7* Chapter 4 'Decimals, percentage and ratio' sections 4.4 and 4.5.

For online help, go to your *Pearson Mathematics 7* eBook.

1 Calculate:

$2.146 + 7.853 + 3.05$

2 Calculate:

$9.6877 - 2.0085$

3 Adele bought the following items at the supermarket.

Eggs	\$3.65
Milk	\$1.80
Cereal	\$7.25
Chocolate bar	\$1.55

How much did she spend in total?

4 Jacob's backpack weighed 10.1 kg. He took out two textbooks, which together weighed 3.5 kg, and also his sports gear, which weighed 1.9 kg. How much did the backpack weigh now?

5 Calculate:

9.514×4

6 Calculate:

0.415×1000

7 Calculate:

15.32×280

8 Calculate:

0.85×0.6

9 Calculate:

5.82×0.624

10 Calculate:

0.8003×0.31

Practice 4B mark: /10

  ISBN 978 1 4886 1399 9

Pearson Mathematics 7 Homework Program

Decimals, percentage and ratio

Skills 4C

Skills & Practice: Total marks /27

Name: ....

Class: ....

Teacher: ....

This side of this worksheet reviews number skills. The other side of this worksheet refers to *Pearson Mathematics 7* Chapter 4 'Decimals, percentage and ratio' sections 4.6, 4.7 and 4.8.

1 Complete the table below:

	-6	9	-4	7	-12	2	-11	5	-8
+ 12									

2 Complete the table below:

	72	132	96	60	144	48	108	36	84
÷ 12									

3 Evaluate 444 000 ÷ 1000.

4 Evaluate 694 × 72.

5 What are the next three numbers in the sequence?

103, 94, 85, 76, …

6 What is the highest common factor of 24 and 64?

7 Calculate (3 + 5) ÷ (3 + 1).

8 Calculate $\frac{7}{8} - \frac{1}{2}$.

9 Insert a <, = or > symbol to make the statement true.

$\frac{22}{10}$ ☐ $1\frac{2}{5}$

10 What is 90% of 200 kg?

11 Find 2.4 ÷ 6.

12 Evaluate $\sqrt{1}$.

13 If 5 + ◆ = 20, find the value of ◆.

14 If ● = 10, what is the value of the expression 3 × (● – 5) + 1?

15 Is a triangle with the three angles 60°, 40° and 80° an obtuse-angled triangle, an acute-angled triangle or a right-angled triangle?

16 A class was surveyed on how much television they had watched the night before, to the nearest hour. What was the most common number of hours of television watched?

Hours of TV	Frequency
0	2
1	9
2	2
3 or more	1
Total	**24**

17 What is the perimeter (in metres) of a rectangular sandpit with length 2.1 m and width 1.6 m?

Skills 4C mark: /17

ISBN 978 1 4886 1399 9

Pearson Mathematics Homework Program 7

Decimals, percentage and ratio

Practice 4C

Show all your working

This side of this worksheet covers *Pearson Mathematics 7* Chapter 4 'Decimals, percentage and ratio' sections 4.6, 4.7 and 4.8.

For online help, go to your *Pearson Mathematics 7* eBook.

1 Calculate:

$5.9544 \div 4$

2 Calculate:

$30.233 \div 7000$

3 Calculate:

$4.2 \div 0.003$

4 A Year 7 class has a stall selling chocolate bars. Before the stall opens they have $32.50 in 50-cent coins. How many 50-cent coins do they have?

5 Write 32% as a fraction in simplest form.

6 Write 74% as a decimal.

7 Write 0.93 as a percentage.

8 Tabia buys a book on sale that normally sells for $32. She gets a 15% discount. How much does she save on the book?

9 Write the following fraction as a percentage.

$\frac{3}{5}$

10 Write the following as a percentage (to 2 decimal places).

$\frac{13}{60}$

Practice 4C mark: /10

  ISBN 978 1 4886 1399 9

Pearson Mathematics 7 Homework Program

Decimals, percentage and ratio

Skills 4D

Skills & Practice: Total marks /27

Name: ....

Class: ....

Teacher: ....

This side of this worksheet reviews number skills. The other side of this worksheet refers to *Pearson Mathematics 7* Chapter 4 'Decimals, percentage and ratio' sections 4.9 and 4.10.

1 Complete the table below:

	12	10	6	7	8	4	2	11	5
× 6									

2 Complete the table below:

	49	70	28	35	14	56	63	84	21
÷ 7									

3 Find 768×1000.

4 Calculate $462 \div 3$.

5 What are the next three numbers in the sequence?

16, 9, 3, -2, …

6 Which of the following numbers are prime?

2, 13, 15, 17, 27, 29

7 Calculate $-5 + 3 \times 15$.

8 Calculate $\frac{4}{5} - \frac{3}{4}$.

9 Which fraction is larger?

$\frac{6}{7}$ or $\frac{7}{8}$

10 Find 20% of \$430.

11 Calculate 0.03×0.7.

12 Evaluate $\sqrt[3]{64}$.

13 If $x + 9 = -1$, find the value of x.

14 If $y = -2$, what is the value of the expression $7 + y$?

15 How many sides does a pentagon have?

16 What is the probability of rolling a prime number on a standard six-sided die?

17 If a square has an area of 25 m^2, what is its perimeter?

Skills 4D mark: /17

ISBN 978 1 4886 1399 9

Pearson Mathematics 7 Homework Program

Decimals, percentage and ratio

Practice 4D

Show all your working

This side of this worksheet covers *Pearson Mathematics 7* Chapter 4 'Decimals, percentage and ratio' sections 4.9 and 4.10.

For online help, go to your *Pearson Mathematics 7* eBook.

1 There are 5 rats, 6 mice and 9 guinea pigs. (Rats, mice and guinea pigs are all 'rodents'.)

Write a ratio for the number of mice to rats.

2 Using the information from the previous question, write a ratio for the number of guinea pigs to the number of rodents.

3 Write an equivalent ratio to 1:4 by multiplying each side of the ratio by 20.

4 Simplify the ratio 6:60.

5 There are 12 dogs and 16 cats at an animal rescue centre. Write this as a ratio of cats to dogs.

6 What fraction of the animals in the previous question is dogs?

7 If 10 litres of orange juice costs $8, how much should 6 litres cost?

8 A car is travelling at a constant speed of 80 km/h. How far will it travel in 45 minutes?

9 A packet of 12 birthday cards costs $7.20. How much does one birthday card cost?

10 At the supermarket there are two options for buying chocolate.
Option A: 400 g for $2.80
Option B: 620 g for $4.96
Which option is the better value?

Practice 4D mark: /10

ISBN 978 1 4886 1399 9

Pearson Mathematics 7 Homework Program

Algebra

Skills 5A

Skills & Practice: Total marks /27

Name:

Class:

Teacher:

This side of this worksheet reviews number skills. The other side of this worksheet refers to *Pearson Mathematics 7* Chapter 5 'Algebra' sections 5.1, 5.2 and 5.3.

1 Complete the table below:

	6	12	7	3	8	4	9	5	11
× 2									

2 Complete the table below:

	16	4	18	8	22	12	24	20	6
÷ 2									

3 Find $27 \times 10\,000$.

4 Calculate 261×64.

5 What are the next two numbers in the sequence?

$\frac{1}{2}, \frac{2}{3}, \frac{3}{4}, \frac{4}{5}, \ldots$

6 List all the common factors of 20 and 36.

7 Find $7 - (-4)$.

8 Calculate $1\frac{2}{3} + \frac{1}{2}$.

9 Which of these decimals are less than a half?

0.048, 0.52, 0.408, 0.84

10 Find 100% of $350.

11 Calculate $0.91 - 0.23$.

12 Evaluate 11^2.

13 If $12 \times \triangle = 36$, find the value of $\triangle$.

14 If ☎ = 6, what is the value of the expression 12 ÷ ☎ − 1?

15 If you are facing east and you turn 270° clockwise, in which direction are you now facing?

16 There are 10 milk chocolates, 6 white chocolates and 4 dark chocolates in a box. What is the largest number of chocolates you could take from the box before you get a white chocolate?

17 How many days are in 5 weeks?

Skills 5A mark: /17

ISBN 978 1 4886 1399 9

Pearson Mathematics 7 Homework Program

Algebra

Practice 5A

Show all your working

This side of this worksheet covers *Pearson Mathematics 7* Chapter 5 'Algebra' sections 5.1, 5.2 and 5.3.

For online help, go to your *Pearson Mathematics 7* eBook.

1 There are k lollipops in one packet, which must be divided equally among a Year 7 class of 25 students. Write an algebraic expression to represent the number of lollipops for each student.

2 Write an algebraic expression for the following situation.

'The sum of f and 2 is multiplied by 3.'

3 Raphael borrowed b books from the library and then borrowed 5 more. Write an algebraic expression to represent the number of books he borrowed in total.

4 Is $5x + 2y$ a term, an expression or an equation?

5 Write a rule to represent the following word problem.

'A certain number is multiplied by 5 and then 4 is added to it.'

6 Write a rule to represent the following word problem.

'A certain number is doubled and then has three times another number subtracted from it.'

7 For the following rule, draw a flowchart, then write the rule using algebra and complete the table of values.

'To get y, multiply x by 2 and then subtract 1.'

x	0	3	2	6	4
y					

8 Write a rule for this flowchart.

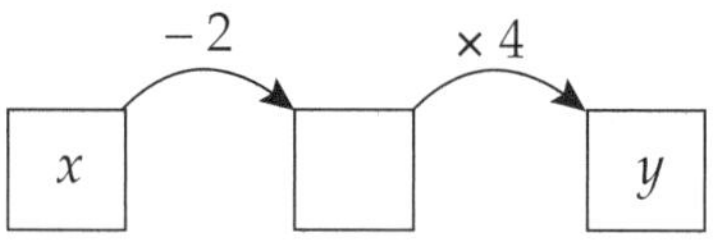

9 Draw a flowchart for this rule.

$y = \frac{x}{2} + 4$

10 Write the following using algebraic notation.
'Add 5 to x and then multiply by 4 to get y.'

Practice 5A mark: /10

ISBN 978 1 4886 1399 9

Pearson Mathematics 7 Homework Program

Algebra

Skills 5B

Skills & Practice: Total marks /25

Name: ....

Class: ....

Teacher: ....

This side of this worksheet reviews number skills. The other side of this worksheet refers to *Pearson Mathematics 7* Chapter 5 'Algebra' sections 5.4, 5.5 and 5.6.

1 Complete the table below:

	-5	8	-12	6	9	-3	11	-7	4
− 6									

2 Complete the table below:

	72	42	30	54	48	12	18	66	36
÷ 6									

3 Find 300 000 ÷ 10 000.

4 Calculate 658 × 72.

5 What are the next two numbers in the sequence?

2, 4, 8, 16, 32, …

6 Express 90 as a product of its prime factors in index form.

7 Insert a < or > symbol to make the statement true.

-6 ☐ 0

8 Calculate $\frac{3}{7} \times \frac{7}{9}$.

9 What is 0.4267 rounded to 3 decimal places?

10 George was sick and away from school for 3 of the last 50 days. What is this as a percentage?

11 Calculate 10.6 + 5.7.

12 Find 3^3.

13 If $22 - n = 12$, find the value of n.

14 If $x = 6$, what is the value of the expression $4(x - 2) + 1$?

15 Is a triangle with the three angles 100°, 40° and 40° an obtuse-angled triangle, an acute-angled triangle or a right-angled triangle?

16 In the last four basketball games, Talia scored 10 points, 8 points, 2 points and 4 points. What was her average score for the four games?

17 What is the area (in m^2) of a tennis court that is 10 m long and 8 m wide?

Skills 5B mark: /17

Algebra

Practice 5B

Show all your working

This side of this worksheet covers *Pearson Mathematics 7* Chapter 5 'Algebra' sections 5.4, 5.5 and 5.6.

For online help, go to your *Pearson Mathematics 7* eBook.

1 Find the value of y if $y = 2x - 3$ and $x = 5$.

2 The perimeter of a rectangle is given by the formula $P = 2L + 2W$ where L = length and W = width. What is the perimeter of a rectangle that has length 5 cm and width 3 cm?

3 Use the rule $y = 3(x - 1) + 2$ to complete this table:

x	1	4	7	9	11
y					

4 A tiler is using tiles on the floor of a bathroom to make a diamond shape.

Size (s)	**1**	**2**	**3**
Diagram			
Number of tiles (m)	4	8	

How many tiles are needed to make a size 3 diamond and a size 4 diamond?

5 From the previous question, find a rule that relates the size of the diamond to the number of tiles needed.

6 Simplify:

$2a + 5a$

7 Simplify:

$4c + 5b - 3c$

8 Simplify:

$12f + 2g + 5g - 3f$

Practice 5B mark: /8

ISBN 978 1 4886 1399 9

Pearson Mathematics 7 Homework Program

Algebra

Skills 5C

Skills & Practice: Total marks /27

Name:

Class:

Teacher:

This side of this worksheet reviews number skills. The other side of this worksheet refers to *Pearson Mathematics 7* Chapter 5 'Algebra' sections 5.7, 5.8 and 5.9.

1 Complete the table below:

	12	6	9	3	11	7	4	8	5
$\times 9$									

2 Complete the table below:

	36	90	72	108	81	54	18	45	27
$\div 9$									

3 Evaluate 5424×100.

4 Calculate 912×30.

5 What are the next three numbers in the sequence?

2, 5, 9, 14, 20, …

6 Find the lowest common multiple of 12 and 9.

7 Calculate $-2 + -3 - 4 - -5$.

8 Find $\frac{3}{4} - \frac{1}{3}$.

9 Write this list in descending order.

$\frac{1}{2}, \frac{1}{3}, \frac{1}{4}, \frac{5}{6}, -\frac{3}{8}$

10 What is 25% of 800 m?

11 Calculate $1.2 \div 3$.

12 Evaluate $\sqrt{49}$.

13 If $h - 11 = 16$, find the value of h.

14 Simplify $2x + 3x$.

15 What is the complement of 35°?

16 Tomio asked eight of his friends how many pets they had. Their responses were 0, 2, 1, 2, 3, 1, 3, 2. What was the most common response?

17 What is the volume (in cm^3) of a cubic six-sided die that has side lengths of 2 cm?

Skills 5C mark: /17

ISBN 978 1 4886 1399 9

Pearson Mathematics 7 Homework Program

Algebra

Practice 5C

This side of this worksheet covers *Pearson Mathematics 7* Chapter 5 'Algebra' sections 5.7, 5.8 and 5.9.

For online help, go to your *Pearson Mathematics 7* eBook.

1 What are the coordinates of point B?

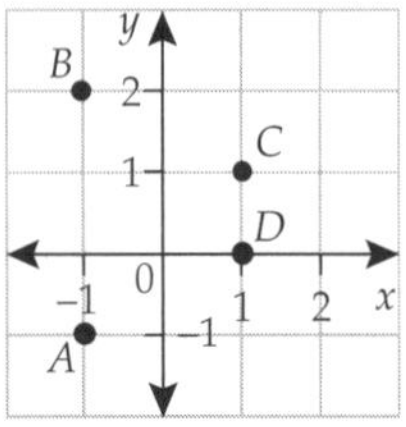

2 In the previous question, which points have the same x-coordinate?

3 Use the graph to discover a special type of number. Write the letters that match the listed points in the order given:
(-1, 1), (1, -2), (-2, 1), (-3, 2), (-2, -1)

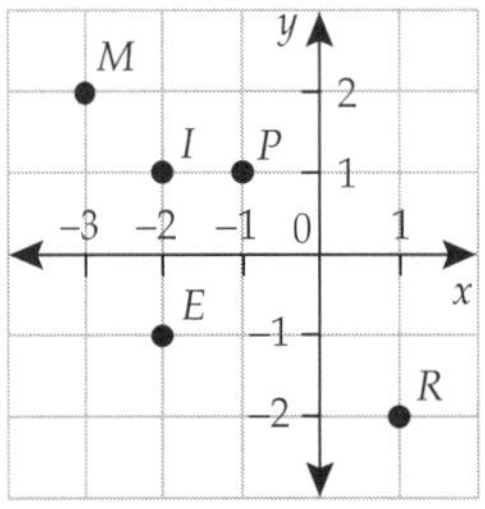

4 Plot the points $A(-3, -2)$, $B(-2, -1)$ and $C(0, 1)$ on the number plane.

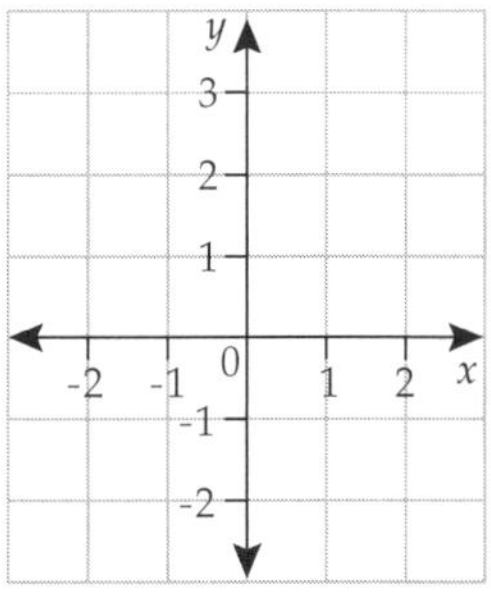

5 A line segment is drawn between the points in the previous question. What are the coordinates of another point that the line also goes through?

6 If the line drawn in the previous question is extended, what are the coordinates of another point that the line will go through? (Choose a point that is on the grid.)

7 Summarise the set of points from Question 4 in the table.

x			
y			

8 Write the rule connecting the x and y values in Question 4.

9 Using the following graph, state which dog is the youngest.

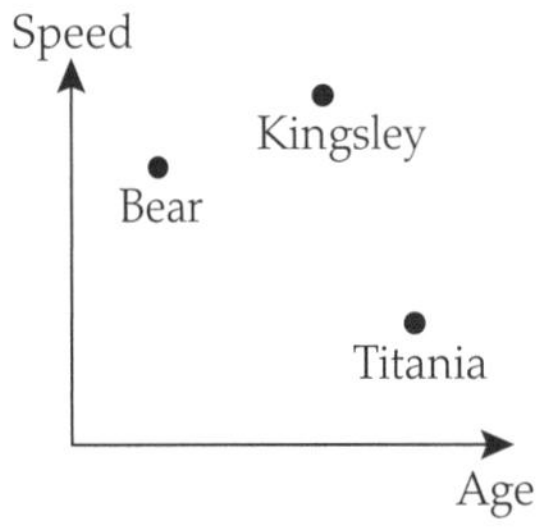

10 Referring to the graph in the previous question, which of the following statements is false?

A Kingsley is older than Bear.
B Titania is the slowest.
C Bear is faster than Kingsley.
D Titania is older than Kingsley.

Practice 5C mark: /10

  ISBN 978 1 4886 1399 9

Pearson Mathematics 7 Homework Program

Measurement

Skills 6A

Skills & Practice: Total marks /27

Name: ....

Class: ....

Teacher: ....

This side of this worksheet reviews number skills. The other side of this worksheet refers to *Pearson Mathematics 7* Chapter 6 'Measurement' sections 6.1 and 6.2.

1 Complete the table below:

	-5	7	-11	6	-9	4	10	-8	12
+ 4									

2 Complete the table below:

	12	40	28	80	48	120	16	24	32
÷ 4									

3 Evaluate 2730×100.

4 Calculate 673×21.

5 What are the next three numbers in the sequence?

3, 9, 15, 21, …

6 Which of these is not a factor of 8?

1, 2, 4, 8, 16

7 Find $(6 - 2) \div (4 - 2)$.

8 Evaluate $\frac{2}{5} + \frac{1}{10}$.

9 Which of these fractions are less than a half?

$\frac{3}{4}, \frac{5}{9}, \frac{4}{8}, \frac{1}{3}, \frac{3}{7}$

10 Find 10% of \$3500.

11 Calculate $0.61 - 0.53$.

12 Evaluate 5^2.

13 If $5 \times \triangle = 35$, find the value of $\triangle$.

14 If $x = 7$, what is the value of the expression $3x - 1$?

15 If you are facing south and you turn 90° clockwise, in which direction are you now facing?

16 What is the probability of rolling an even number using a standard six-sided die?

17 It is 10:22 am now and I am meeting a friend after school at 3:35 pm. How many minutes until I meet her?

Skills 6A mark: /17

ISBN 978 1 4886 1399 9

Pearson Mathematics 7 Homework Program

Measurement

Practice 6A

Show all your working

This side of this worksheet covers *Pearson Mathematics 7* Chapter 6 'Measurement' sections 6.1 and 6.2.

For online help, go to your *Pearson Mathematics 7* eBook.

1 Which unit of length would be most suitable for measuring how far a person can jump?

2 How many centimetres are in 210 mm?

3 Convert 2400 cm to kilometres.

4 A group of hikers walk 3.4 km in the morning and 1300 m in the afternoon. What is the total distance they walk in kilometres?

5 Some bricks are 18 cm long. If a wall is made up of 50 of these bricks placed lengthways, how long is the wall in metres?

6 Sam buys a 1-metre roll of licorice. How many 5 cm lengths can it be cut into?

7 Find the perimeter of a rectangle that has width 17 mm and length 2 cm.

8 Find the perimeter of this shape (in millimetres).

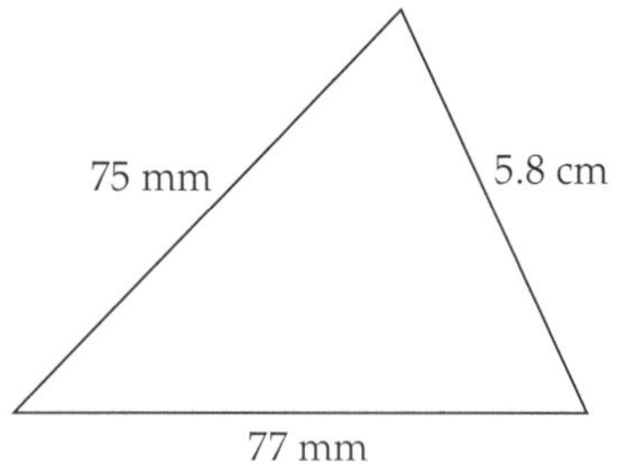

9 Find the perimeter of this shape.

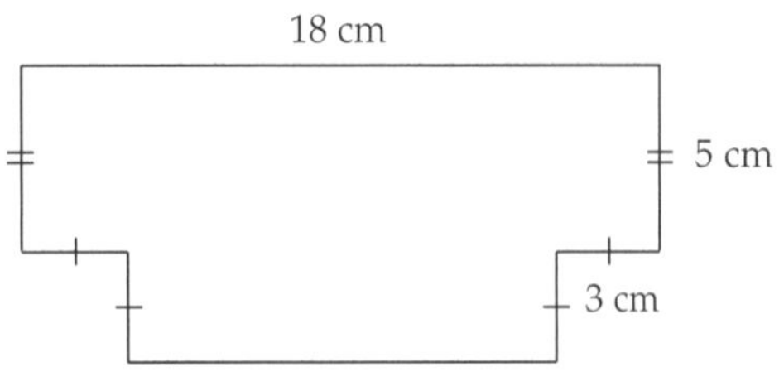

10 A soccer team runs 4 times around a rectangular gym as part of their warm-up. The gym is 65 m long and 40 m wide. What distance does the team run?

Practice 6A mark: /10

ISBN 978 1 4886 1399 9

Pearson Mathematics 7 Homework Program

Measurement

Skills 6B

Skills & Practice: Total marks /27

Name:

Class:

Teacher:

This side of this worksheet reviews number skills. The other side of this worksheet refers to *Pearson Mathematics 7* Chapter 6 'Measurement' sections 6.3 and 6.4.

1 Complete the table below:

	5	7	11	6	9	4	10	8	12
× 7									

2 Complete the table below:

	77	21	35	7	140	42	700	49	280
÷ 7									

3 Evaluate 9000 ÷100.

4 Calculate 611 × 18.

5 What are the next three numbers in the sequence?

1, 3, 9, 27, …

6 Which of these are multiples of 9?

3, 27, 1, 99, 9

7 Find -1 + 7 – (-4).

8 Calculate $\frac{3}{8} \times \frac{4}{9}$.

9 What is 0.426 rounded to 2 decimal places?

10 I have $120 in savings. If I give 20% of this to a charity, how much have I donated?

11 Calculate 2.53 + 5.49.

12 Evaluate 1^3.

13 If $19 - y = 12$, find the value of y.

14 Simplify ☺ + ◇ + ☺ – ☺ + ☺ + ◇.

15 What is the value of the angle a in this diagram?

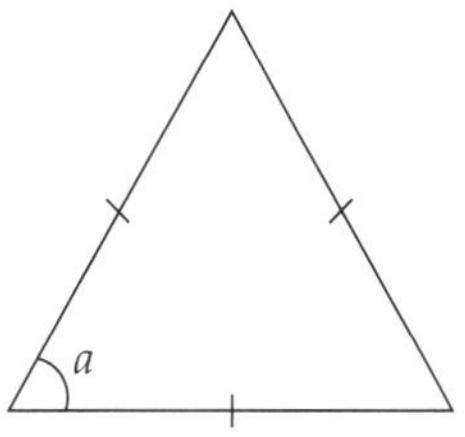

16 In a box there are 10 milk chocolates, 5 white chocolates and 5 dark chocolates. If you take a chocolate at random, what is the probability that it is a white chocolate?

17 How many millimetres are in 4.1 m?

Skills 6B mark: /17

ISBN 978 1 4886 1399 9

Pearson Mathematics 7 Homework Program

Measurement

Practice 6B

Show all your working

This side of this worksheet covers *Pearson Mathematics 7* Chapter 6 'Measurement' sections 6.3 and 6.4.

For online help, go to your *Pearson Mathematics 7* eBook.

1 Which unit of area would be most suitable for measuring the area of your bedroom?

2 Which unit of area would be best for measuring the area of a 20-cent coin?

3 Imagine the shape below is drawn on centimetre grid paper. Find its area.

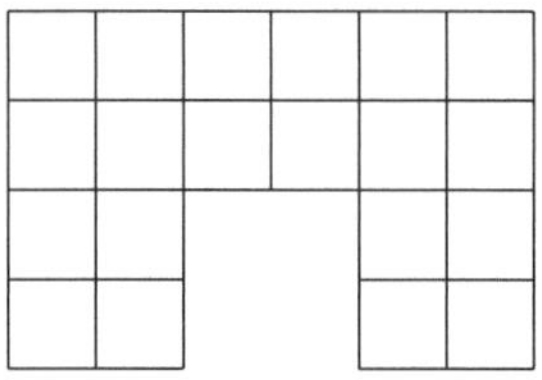

4 Find the area of this square.

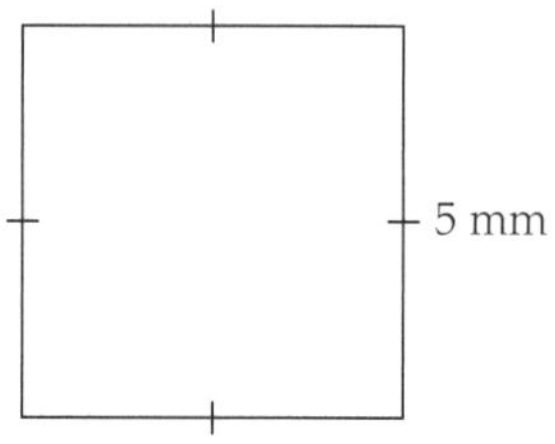

5 Find the area of a rectangle of length 12 m and width 7 m.

6 Garrison wants to weed his rectangular garden. He can weed approximately 4 m^2 every 15 minutes. If his garden is 8 m long and 1.5 m wide, how much time will it take him to weed the garden?

7 If a rectangle has an area of 36 cm^2 and a width of 3 cm, what is its length?

8 Find the area of this parallelogram.

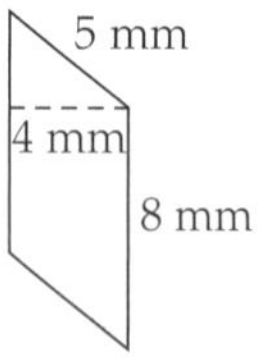

9 Find the area of this parallelogram.

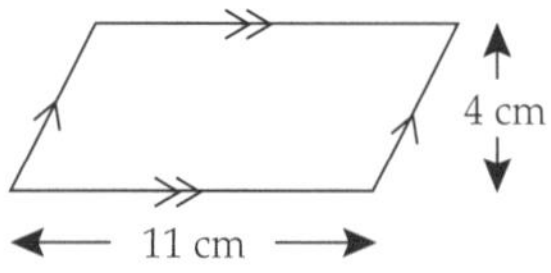

10 A parallelogram has an area of 240 cm^2. What is its height if the base length is 20 cm?

Practice 6B mark: /10

ISBN 978 1 4886 1399 9

Pearson Mathematics 7 Homework Program

Measurement

Skills 6C

Skills & Practice: Total marks /27

Name: ....

Class: ....

Teacher: ....

This side of this worksheet reviews number skills. The other side of this worksheet refers to *Pearson Mathematics 7* Chapter 6 'Measurement' sections 6.5 and 6.6.

1 Complete the table below:

	5	7	11	6	9	4	10	8	12
× 12									

2 Complete the table below:

	120	36	12	240	48	108	72	132	60
÷ 12									

3 Evaluate 432×100.

4 Calculate 217×42.

5 What are the next three numbers in the sequence?

3, 8, 15, 24, …

6 Which of these numbers are prime?

11, 12, 13, 14, 15, 16, 17

7 Write these numbers in descending order.

-3, 0, -1, 3, 5, -4

8 Calculate $1\frac{3}{4} - \frac{1}{2}$.

9 Insert a < or > symbol to make the statement true.

$\frac{6}{11}$ ☐ $\frac{6}{10}$

10 What is 20% of 500 g?

11 Calculate $3.2 \div 8$.

12 Evaluate $\sqrt{25}$.

13 If $a - 7 = 16$, find the value of a.

14 If ☺ = 3, what is the value of the expression $3 \times (5 - ☺) + 1$?

15 How many sides does a hexagon have?

16 The results of a class survey to find the favourite type of chocolate are given in the table.

Chocolate	Frequency
White	7
Milk	15
Dark	2
None	1
Total	**25**

What was the most popular chocolate?

17 How many square centimetres are in 2 m^2?

Skills 6C mark: /17

ISBN 978 1 4886 1399 9

Pearson Mathematics Homework Program 7

Measurement

Practice 6C

Show all your working

This side of this worksheet covers *Pearson Mathematics 7* Chapter 6 'Measurement' sections 6.5 and 6.6.

For online help, go to your *Pearson Mathematics 7* eBook.

1 Find the area of a triangle with a base length of 20 cm and a height of 8 cm.

2 Find the area of this triangle.

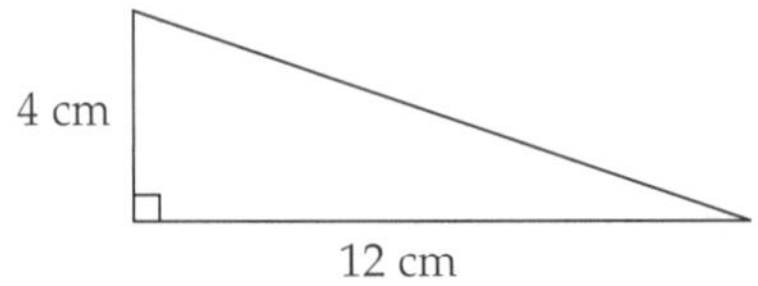

3 Find the area of this triangle.

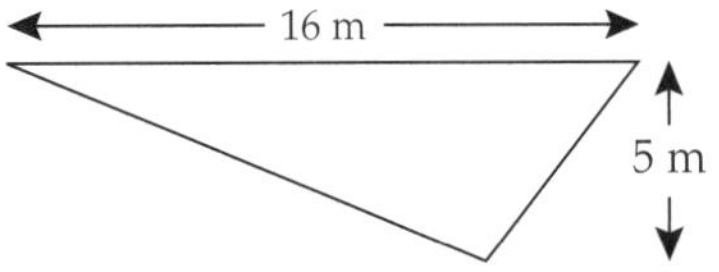

4 Calculate the area of this composite shape.

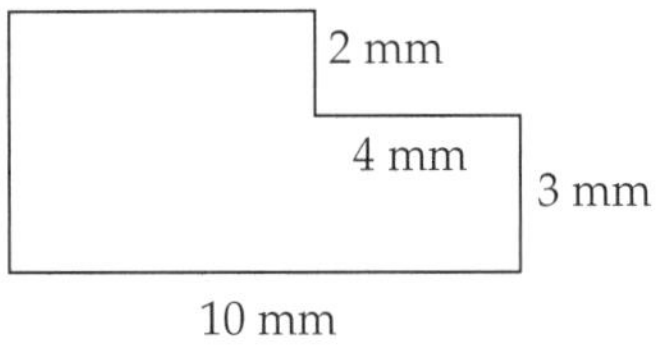

5 Calculate the area of this composite shape.

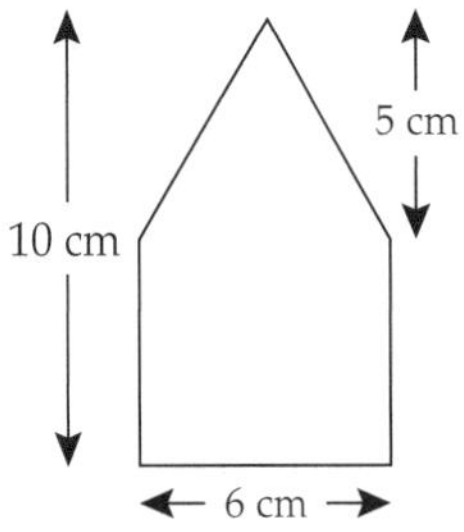

6 Calculate the area of this composite shape.

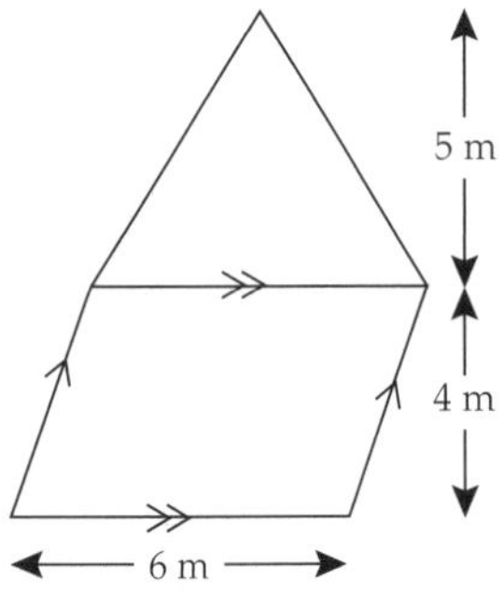

7 Find the volume of the stack of centimetre cubes pictured below.

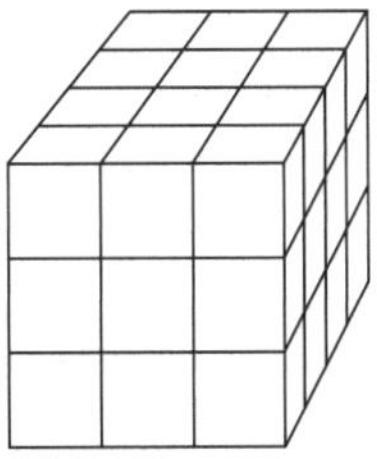

8 Calculate the volume of the prism below.

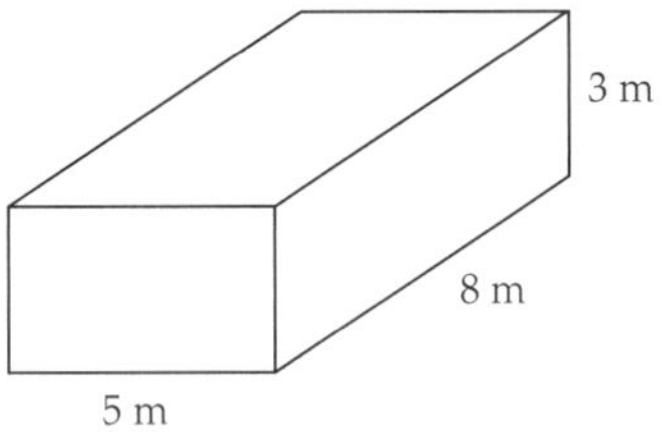

9 A rectangular swimming pool has a depth of 2 m and is 5 m wide and 11 m long. What is its volume?

10 A rectangular box has a height of 10 cm, width of 8 cm and volume of 960 cm^3.
What is its length?

Practice 6C mark: /10

  ISBN 978 1 4886 1399 9

Pearson Mathematics 7 Homework Program

Linear equations

Skills 7A

Skills & Practice: Total marks /27

Name:

Class:

Teacher:

This side of this worksheet reviews number skills. The other side of this worksheet refers to *Pearson Mathematics 7* Chapter 7 'Linear equations' sections 7.1 and 7.2.

1 Complete the table below:

	5	-12	9	-6	8	-3	11	-7	4
− 8									

2 Complete the table below:

	32	80	56	72	40	64	96	48	16
÷ 8									

3 Evaluate 549×1000.

4 Calculate 851×32.

5 What are the next two numbers in the sequence?

121, 151, 181, 211, …

6 List all the factors of 72 in ascending order.

7 Calculate $6 \div 3 + 2 \times 1$.

8 Find $\frac{1}{3} + \frac{4}{9}$.

9 Which of these fractions are greater than 1?

$\frac{3}{4}, \frac{10}{9}, \frac{8}{8}, 1\frac{1}{3}, \frac{6}{7}$

10 Find 2% of \$400.

11 Calculate $12.6 - 5.8$.

12 Evaluate 6^2.

13 If $4 \times f = 36$, find the value of f.

14 If $k = 3$, what is the value of the expression $4k - 1$?

15 Is a triangle with the angles 50°, 40° and 90° an obtuse-angled triangle, an acute-angled triangle or a right-angled triangle?

16 What is the probability of picking a red card from a standard pack of 52 playing cards?

17 Fran has to get up for school at 7:30 am. How much sleep can she get if it is 9:45 pm now and she falls straight to sleep?

Skills 7A mark: /17

ISBN 978 1 4886 1399 9

Pearson Mathematics Homework Program 7

Linear equations

Practice 7A

Show all your working

This side of this worksheet covers *Pearson Mathematics 7* Chapter 7 'Linear equations' sections 7.1 and 7.2.

For online help, go to your *Pearson Mathematics 7* eBook.

1 The following number sentence is not true. Change the number in *italics* to make a true number sentence.

$\mathit{10} - 3 = 5$

2 The following number sentence is not true. Change the number in *italics* to make a true number sentence.

$\frac{24}{2} = \mathit{4}$

3 Complete this statement to make a true number sentence.

$5 + \_\_\_ \times 7 = 26$

4 Find the unknown number described below.

'A number is multiplied by 5 and then has 3 added to it. The result is equal to 23.'

5 Find the unknown number described below.

'Jeevan had exactly enough money to buy either three doughnuts at 80 cents each, or six chocolate-chip cookies. How much is each cookie?'

6 Write this equation in words.

$2m + 4 = 12$

7 Write this equation in words.

$\frac{50}{e} = 10$

8 Check to see if the value given in brackets is the solution to the equation.

$2x + 1 = 12 \qquad (x = 5)$

9 Check to see if the value given in brackets is the solution to the equation.

$\frac{a}{5} + 3 = 11 \qquad (a = 40)$

10 Find the solution to this equation.

$\frac{x}{3} + 6 = 14$

Practice 7A mark: /10

ISBN 978 1 4886 1399 9

Pearson Mathematics 7 Homework Program

Linear equations

Skills 7B

Skills & Practice: Total marks /25

Name:

Class:

Teacher:

This side of this worksheet reviews number skills. The other side of this worksheet refers to *Pearson Mathematics 7* Chapter 7 'Linear equations' section 7.3.

1 Complete the table below:

	8	3	6	11	4	9	5	12	7
× 3									

2 Complete the table below:

	21	6	24	12	36	18	9	27	15
÷ 3									

3 Evaluate $9700 \div 100$.

4 Calculate 835×24.

5 What are the next two numbers in the sequence?

1, 4, 9, 16, 25, …

6 What is the next prime number after 80?

7 While climbing a snow-covered mountain, the climber observed that the temperature dropped from 12 °C to -13 °C. By how many degrees did the temperature drop?

8 Find $\frac{5}{6} \times \frac{3}{10}$.

9 What is 10.002 rounded to 2 decimal places?

10 What percentage of the numbers on a standard six-sided die are even?

11 Calculate $0.98 + 0.75$.

12 Evaluate 2^4.

13 If $y - 9 = 21$, find the value of y.

14 Simplify $5w + 3v - 2w$.

15 What is the complement of 60°?

16 For the last seven days Peter played computer games for the following number of hours: 1, 3, 4, 2, 1, 2, 1. What is the average number of hours he played computer games each day?

17 What is the area of the floor of Gina's room, which is 3 m long and 2.2 m wide?

Skills 7B mark: /17

ISBN 978 1 4886 1399 9

Pearson Mathematics 7 Homework Program

Linear equations

Practice 7B

Show all your working

This side of this worksheet covers *Pearson Mathematics 7* Chapter 7 'Linear equations' section 7.3.

For online help, go to your *Pearson Mathematics 7* eBook.

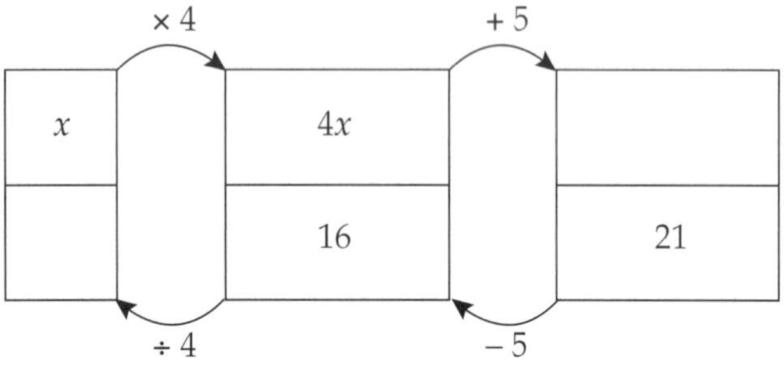

1 Write the equation to be solved for the flowchart on the left.

2 Using the flowchart, find the solution to the equation.

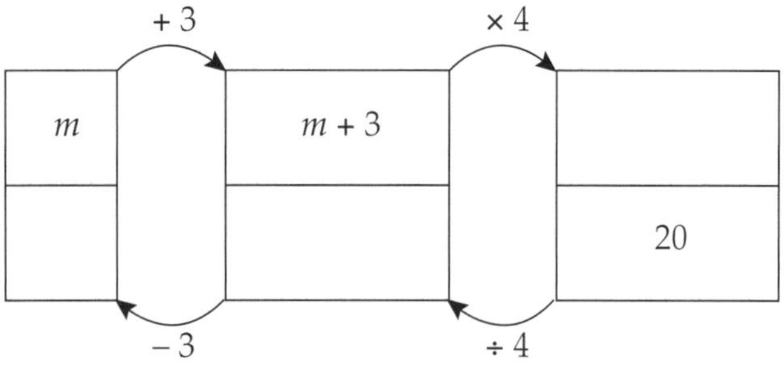

3 Write the equation to be solved for the flowchart on the left.

4 Using the flowchart and backtracking, solve the equation.

5 Use the flowchart provided to solve the equation $9x - 4 = 5$.

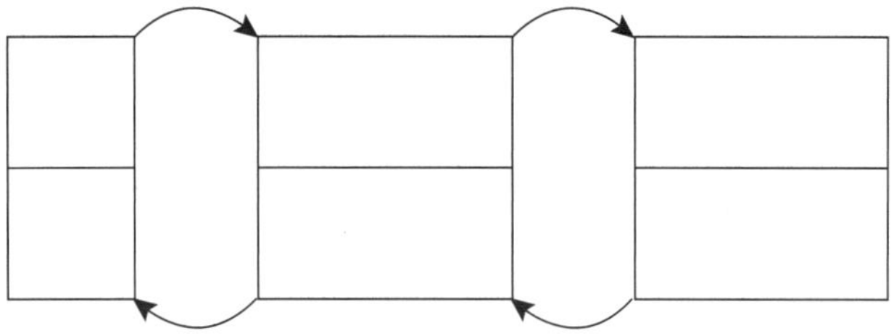

6 Write an equation to describe the following and then solve by backtracking: A number has 1 subtracted from it and then the result is doubled, giving an answer of 8.

7 Solve $\frac{2x}{3} + 4 = 8$ by backtracking.

8 Solve $\frac{2(x+3)}{7} = 2$ by backtracking.

Practice 7B mark: /18

ISBN 978 1 4886 1399 9

Pearson Mathematics 7 Homework Program

Linear equations

Skills 7C

Skills & Practice: Total marks /27

Name:

Class:

Teacher:

This side of this worksheet reviews number skills. The other side of this worksheet refers to *Pearson Mathematics 7* Chapter 7 'Linear equations' sections 7.4 and 7.5.

1 Complete the table below:

	10	2	12	7	4	9	11	6	8
− 5									

2 Complete the table below:

	80	120	100	30	10	90	40	60	110
÷ 10									

3 Evaluate 5310×1000.

4 Find 510×47.

5 What are the next three numbers in the sequence?

$1, \frac{1}{2}, \frac{1}{3}, \frac{1}{4}, \frac{1}{5}, \ldots$

6 List all the common factors of 12 and 18.

7 Calculate $12 \div (6 - 4)$.

8 Calculate $1\frac{3}{4} - \frac{1}{8}$.

9 Insert a < or > symbol to make the statement true.

$\frac{9}{5}$ ☐ $1\frac{6}{10}$

10 What is 50% of 178 minutes?

11 Find 0.9×3.

12 Evaluate $\sqrt{144}$.

13 If $c + 11 = 27$, find the value of c.

14 Simplify $14r + 9s - 5s + 2r$.

15 What is the supplement of 135°?

16 Romeo is running late for school and only has time to grab a pair of socks from his drawer without looking. In the drawer he has 3 pairs of grey school socks, 2 pairs of white socks and 1 pair of black socks. What is the probability that he grabs a pair of grey school socks?

17 What is the volume of Tianna's toddler pool, which is 2 m long, 2 m wide and 0.5 m deep?

Skills 7C mark: /17

ISBN 978 1 4886 1399 9

Pearson Mathematics Homework Program 7

Linear equations

Practice 7C

Show all your working

This side of this worksheet covers *Pearson Mathematics 7* Chapter 7 'Linear equations' sections 7.4 and 7.5.

For online help, go to your *Pearson Mathematics 7* eBook.

1 Write the result of adding 5 to both sides of the equation $5x - 5 = 4x - 2$.

2 Write the result of subtracting 3 from both sides of the equation $2x + 7 = 4$.

3 Write the first operation you must do to both sides of the equation $2x + 3 = 15$ to begin to solve it.

4 Write the first operation you must do to both sides of the equation $3x - 4 = 8$ to begin to solve it.

5 Solve $7x + 1 = 15$ using the balance method.

6 Solve $6x - 5 = 13$ using the balance method.

7 Adel has \$2. He buys a chocolate bar with this and gets 70 cents change. If x is the cost of a chocolate bar, write the equation that can be formed.

8 A packet of stickers is divided equally among eight people. If each person gets 12 stickers and b is the number of stickers in the packet, write the equation that can be formed.

9 Stephanie had \$6 to spend at the football. She bought two mini-buckets of chips and was given change of 60 cents. How much does a mini-bucket of chips cost?

10 Taj's grass-cutting service charges \$20 to attend each job, to cover petrol costs and travel time, plus \$15 per hour for mowing.

If a grass-cutting job cost \$80, how many hours of mowing were done?

Practice 7C mark: /10

  ISBN 978 1 4886 1399 9

Pearson Mathematics 7 Homework Program

Angles and shapes

Skills 8A

Skills & Practice: Total marks /27

Name: ....

Class: ....

Teacher: ....

This side of this worksheet reviews number skills. The other side of this worksheet refers to *Pearson Mathematics 7* Chapter 8 'Angles and shapes' sections 8.1, 8.2 and 8.3.

1 Complete the table below:

	7	2	11	4	8	12	3	9	6
× 12									

2 Complete the table below:

	96	36	108	60	144	72	48	84	132
÷ 12									

3 Evaluate 230×1000.

4 Find 127×96.

5 What are the next two numbers in the sequence?

1, 3, 9, 27, …

6 Find the first five multiples of 9.

7 Calculate $(3 - 4 \div 2) + 5$.

8 Find $\frac{4}{5} + \frac{2}{5}$.

9 Which of these fractions are less than a third?

$\frac{1}{4}, \frac{2}{6}, \frac{2}{5}, \frac{1}{6}, \frac{1}{5}$

10 Find 10% of 400 km.

11 Calculate $6.7 - 0.7$.

12 Find 10^2.

13 If $4 \times \square = 44$, find the value of $\square$.

14 If $\square = 4$, what is the value of the expression $2 \times \square + 3$?

15 If you are facing north and you turn 180° clockwise, in which direction are you now facing?

16 Decide whether you would describe the event 'I will eat some vegetables tomorrow' as 'impossible', 'not likely', 'likely' or 'certain'.

17 How many millimetres are in 1.2 m?

Skills 8A mark: /17

ISBN 978 1 4886 1399 9

Pearson Mathematics Homework Program

7

Angles and shapes

Practice 8A

Show all your working

This side of this worksheet covers *Pearson Mathematics 7* Chapter 8 'Angles and shapes' sections 8.1, 8.2 and 8.3.

For online help, go to your *Pearson Mathematics 7* eBook.

1 Measure this angle using a protractor.

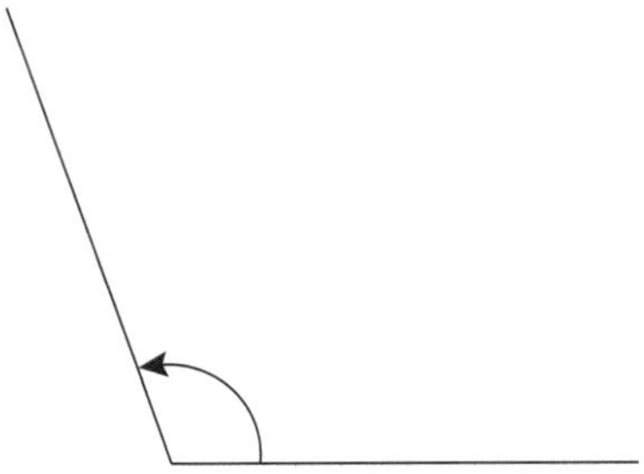

2 Estimate the size of the angle shown.

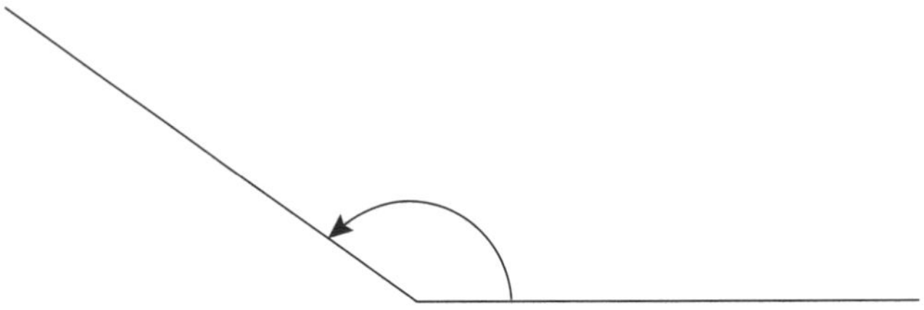

3 Draw an angle of 65°.

4 Classify this angle.

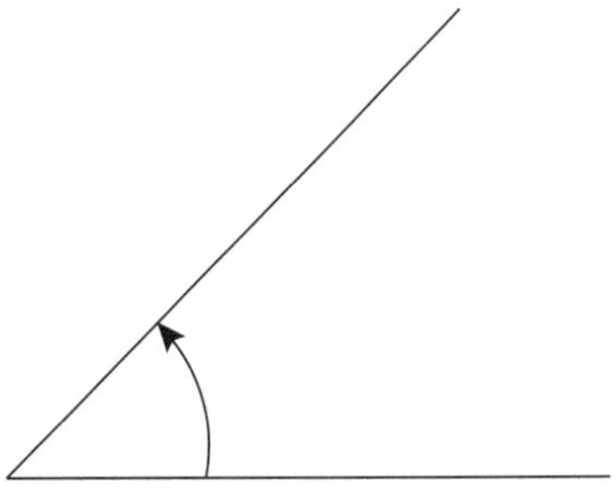

5 Classify this angle.

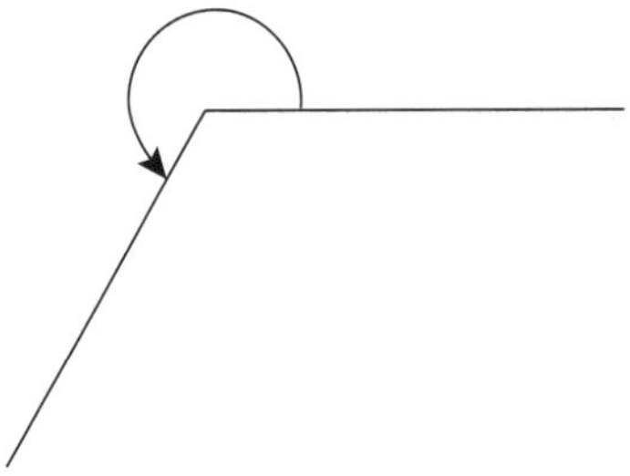

6 Find the size of angle x.

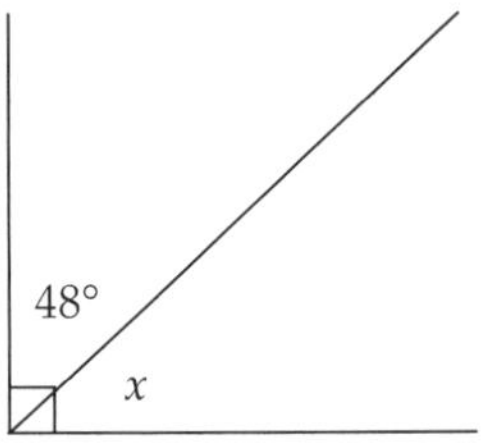

7 What is the complement of 27°?

8 What is the supplement of 63°?

9 Find the size of angle x.

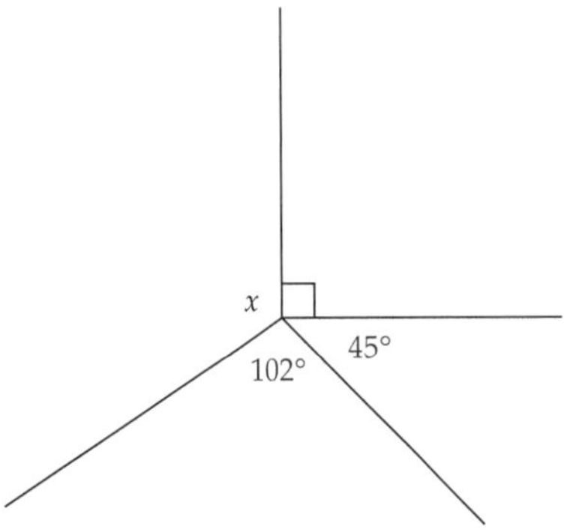

10 Find the size of angle x.

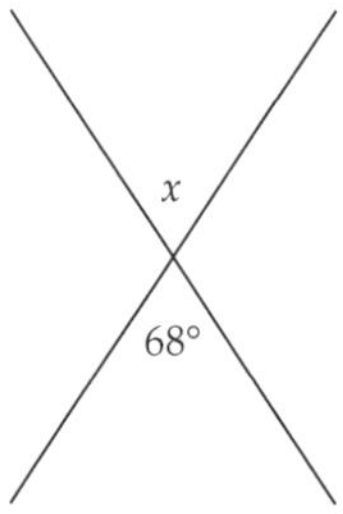

Practice 8A mark: /10

ISBN 978 1 4886 1399 9

Pearson Mathematics 7 Homework Program

Angles and shapes

Skills 8B

Skills & Practice: Total marks /27

Name:

Class:

Teacher:

This side of this worksheet reviews number skills. The other side of this worksheet refers to *Pearson Mathematics 7* Chapter 8 'Angles and shapes' sections 8.4 and 8.5.

1 Complete the table below:

	-8	3	-12	-6	11	-7	-4	-9	5
+ 8									

2 Complete the table below:

	32	96	16	56	72	48	64	88	24
÷ 8									

3 Evaluate 72 000 ÷ 1000.

4 Calculate 831 × 32.

5 What are the next three numbers in the sequence?

5, 4, 6, 5, 7, 6, 8, 7, …

6 List all the factors of 12 in ascending order.

7 Find $4 + (2 + 15 \div 3) \times 2$.

8 Calculate $\frac{2}{3} \times \frac{1}{2}$.

9 What is 1.532 rounded to 2 decimal places?

10 In the last week, Reha was late to school on 2 of the 5 days. What is this as a percentage?

11 Calculate 5.2 + 0.7.

12 Find 4^3.

13 If 12 – ⃠ = 4, find the value of ⃠.

14 If ◇ = 6, what is the value of the expression 3 × (◇ – 2)?

15 Is this angle closer to 100 or 110 degrees?

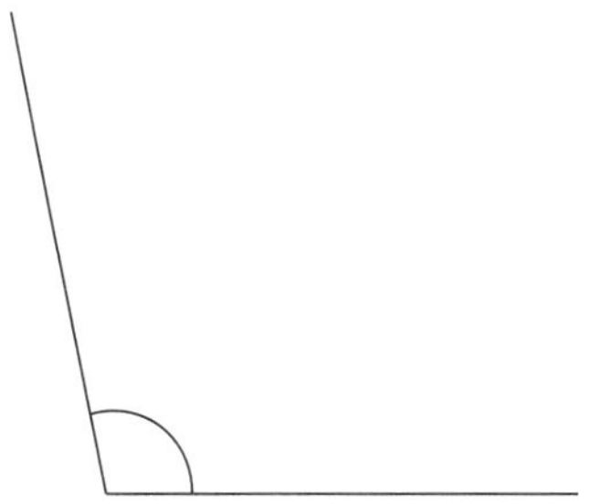

16 What is the probability of rolling a 7 using a standard six-sided die?

17 How many centimetres are in 2 km?

Skills 8B mark: /17

ISBN 978 1 4886 1399 9

Pearson Mathematics Homework Program 7

Angles and shapes

Practice 8B

Show all your working

This side of this worksheet covers *Pearson Mathematics 7* Chapter 8 'Angles and shapes' sections 8.4 and 8.5.

For online help, go to your *Pearson Mathematics 7* eBook.

1 Write the pairs of alternate angles in the following diagram.

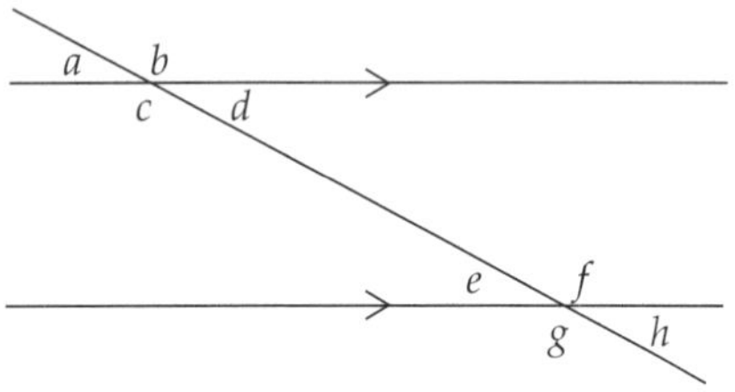

2 In the diagram for Question 1, which angle is the corresponding angle to angle *d*?

3 In the diagram for Question 1, which angle is co-interior to angle *e*?

4 Find the value of angle *c*.

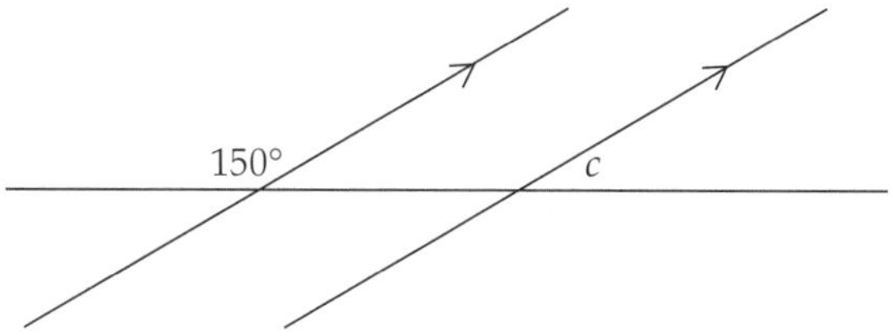

5 Find the value of angle *d*.

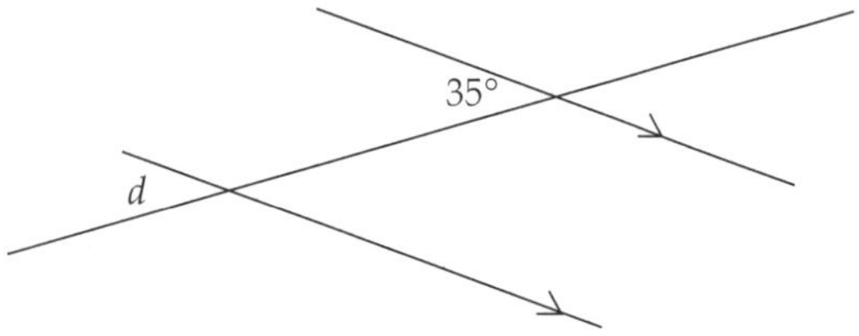

6 Find the value of the unknown angles in the diagram below.

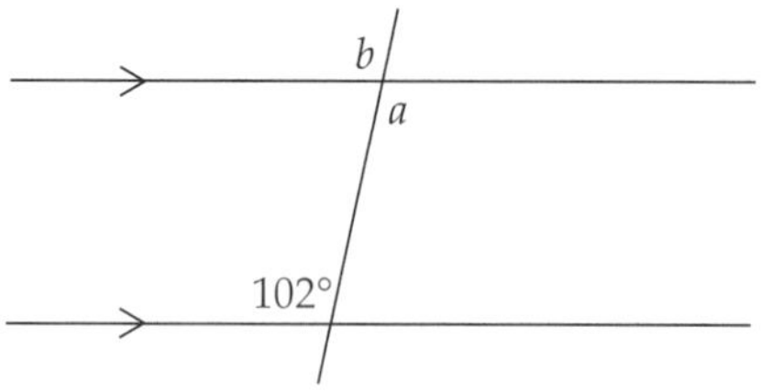

7 State the name of the polygon shown.

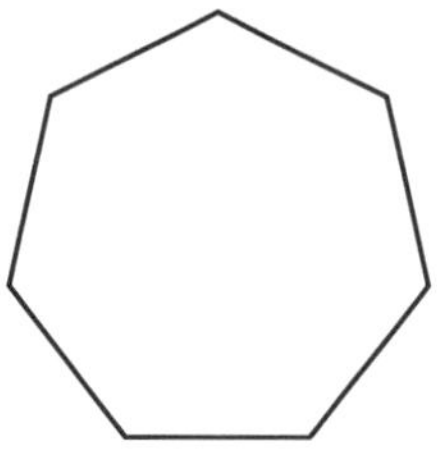

8 State the name of the polygon shown.

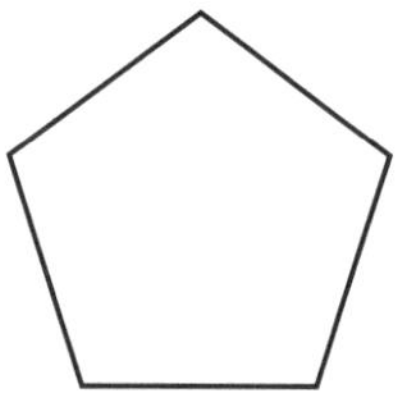

9 Draw an irregular hexagon.

10 Draw a concave octagon.

Practice 8B mark: /10

ISBN 978 1 4886 1399 9

Pearson Mathematics 7 Homework Program

Angles and shapes

Skills 8C

Skills & Practice: Total marks /27

Name: ....

Class: ....

Teacher: ....

This side of this worksheet reviews number skills. The other side of this worksheet refers to *Pearson Mathematics 7* Chapter 8 'Angles and shapes' sections 8.6, 8.7 and 8.8.

1 Complete the table below:

	7	2	5	9	6	12	3	8	4
× 9									

2 Complete the table below:

	54	36	99	27	108	81	72	45	63
÷ 9									

3 Evaluate 320×100.

4 Find 972×54.

5 What are the next three numbers in the sequence?

4, 10, 16, 22, …

6 Which of the factors of 12 are prime numbers?

7 Calculate $15 \div (2 + 3) - 3$.

8 Find $2 - \frac{1}{2}$.

9 Add a < or > symbol to make the statement true.

0.001 [ ] 0.01

10 What is 15% of $100?

11 Find 0.6×8.

12 Evaluate $\sqrt{81}$.

13 If ☎ + 11 = 26, find the value of ☎.

14 If ❁ = 3, what is the value of the expression 4 × (5 − ❁) + 1?

15 Classify this angle.

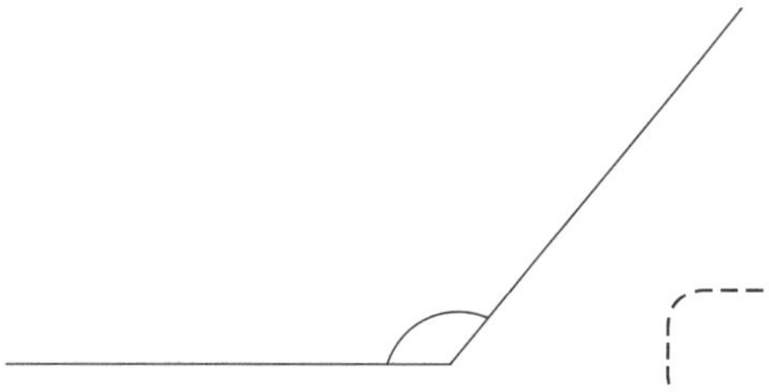

16 Students in five different Year 7 classes were asked how many home computers they had. If 💻 means 10 computers, ⌨ means 5 computers and 🖱 means 1 computer, which class had the most computers in their homes?

Class	Number of computers
7A	💻💻⌨🖱
7B	💻💻⌨🖱🖱
7C	💻⌨🖱🖱🖱🖱
7D	💻💻🖱🖱
7E	💻💻⌨🖱

17 What is the perimeter of a square with side length 7 cm?

Skills 8C mark: /17

ISBN 978 1 4886 1399 9

Pearson Mathematics 7 Homework Program

Angles and shapes

Practice 8C

Show all your working

This side of this worksheet covers *Pearson Mathematics 7* Chapter 8 'Angles and shapes' sections 8.6, 8.7 and 8.8.

For online help, go to your *Pearson Mathematics 7* eBook.

1 Measure the side lengths of the triangle at right and classify it based on these side lengths.

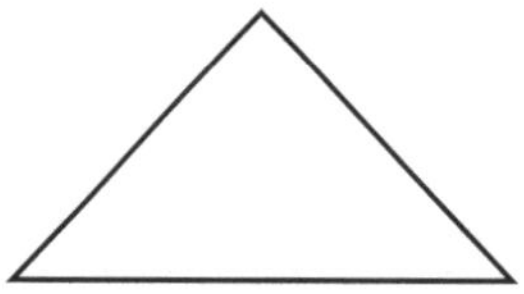

2 Measure the angles of the triangle at right and classify it based on these angles.

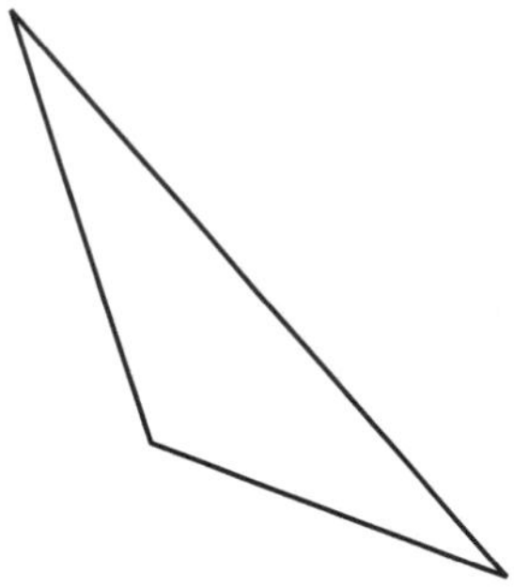

3 Calculate the size of angle *e*.

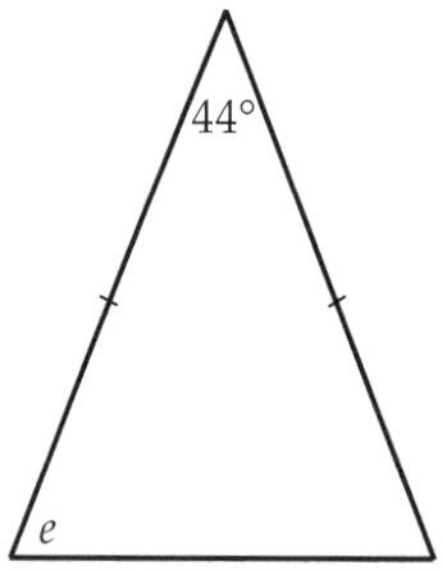

4 Find the size of angle *t* in the triangle below.

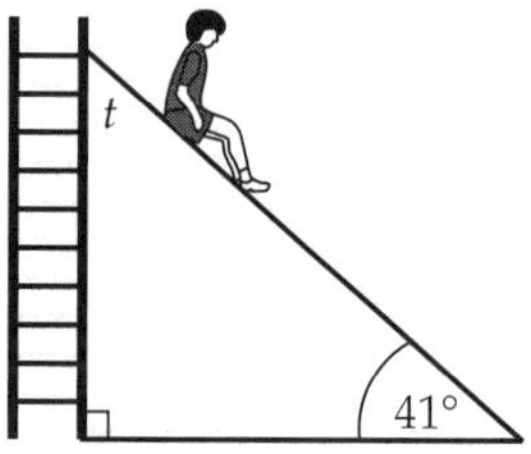

5 Classify this type of shape.

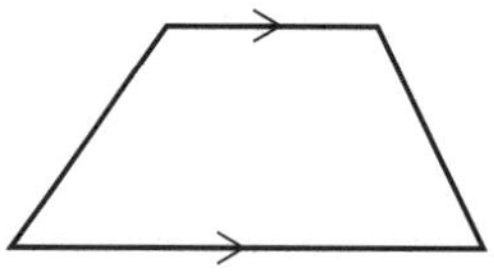

6 Find the size of angle *d* in this triangle.

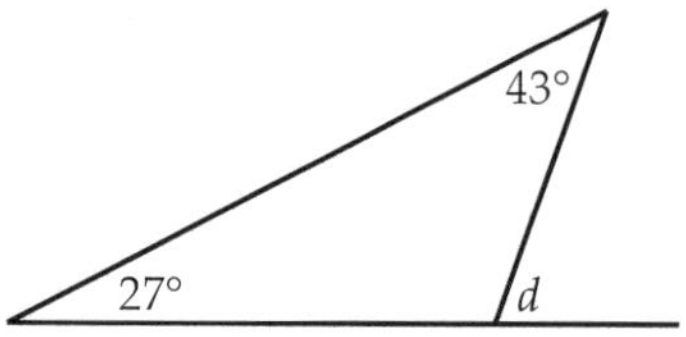

7 Find the size of angle *d* in this quadrilateral.

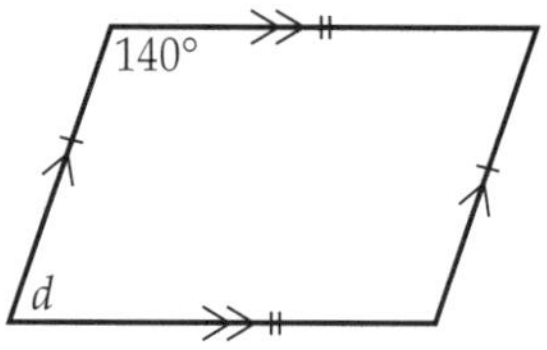

8 Find the size of angle *d* in this quadrilateral.

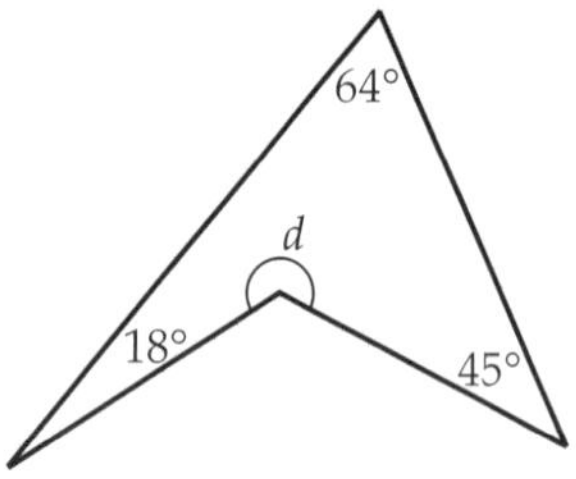

9 A quadrilateral has two angles of 100° and 80°. The other two angles are equal to each other. What is the size of the other two angles?

10 Construct an equilateral triangle using a compass and ruler.

Practice 8C mark: /10

  ISBN 978 1 4886 1399 9

Pearson Mathematics 7 Homework Program

Statistics and probability

Skills 9A

Skills & Practice: Total marks /25

Name:

Class:

Teacher:

This side of this worksheet reviews number skills. The other side of this worksheet refers to *Pearson Mathematics 7* Chapter 9 'Statistics and probability' sections 9.1 and 9.2.

1 Complete the table below:

	3	9	6	12	4	8	11	5	7
× 4									

2 Complete the table below:

	24	48	8	36	28	44	12	32	16
÷ 4									

3 Evaluate 9430×1000.

4 Calculate 396×24.

5 What are the next three numbers in the sequence?

168, 156, 144, 132, 120, …

6 Find the lowest common multiple of 12 and 10.

7 Find $2 \times (3 + 1) \times 4$.

8 Calculate $1\frac{1}{4} + 1\frac{1}{6}$.

9 Simplify the fraction $\frac{25}{200}$.

10 Evaluate 1% of $9500.

11 Find $7.0 - 5.3$.

12 Find 8^2.

13 If $8g = 16$, find the value of g.

14 If $y = 7$, what is the value of the expression $2y - 5$?

15 Find the size of angle d in the quadrilateral.

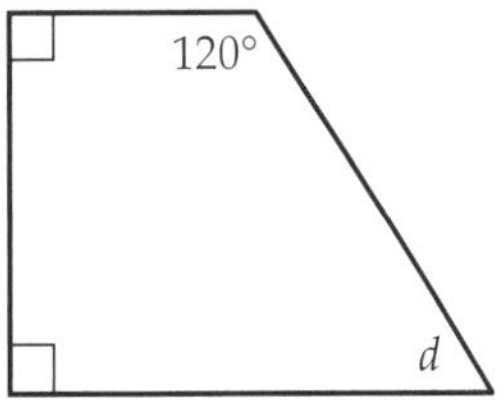

16 What is the probability of getting a black card when you take a card from a standard pack of 52 playing cards?

17 What is the volume of a rectangular lunchbox that is 5 cm high, 20 cm long and 15 cm wide?

Skills 9A mark: /17

ISBN 978 1 4886 1399 9

Pearson Mathematics Homework Program 7

Statistics and probability

Practice 9A

Show all your working

This side of this worksheet covers *Pearson Mathematics 7* Chapter 9 'Statistics and probability' sections 9.1 and 9.2.

For online help, go to your *Pearson Mathematics 7* eBook.

1 A Year 7 class was surveyed to find out how many hamburgers they ate on the weekend. The following results were obtained:

0, 2, 1, 0, 4, 3, 0, 2, 0, 3, 1, 0, 2, 1, 0, 1, 3, 2

Make a frequency table for this survey.

2 Borys worked part-time delivering pamphlets. He earned these amounts (in $):

45, 58, 65, 98, 47, 66, 74, 70, 52, 44,

65, 82, 75, 50, 66, 62, 76, 80, 95, 90

Put this data into a frequency table using intervals of 10, with the first interval 40–49.

3 Find the mode of the data in Question 1. Is the data categorical or numerical?

4 Calculate the mean of these heights (in cm), correct to 2 decimal places.

165, 178, 196, 187, 158, 177

5 Find the median for the data in Question 4.

6 Find the median for this set of test results.

85, 58, 64, 78, 56, 91, 32

7 For each of the following, say whether the data is categorical, discrete or continuous.

a favourite animal
b length of your foot
c number of siblings you have

8 Calculate the mode for the following data.

58, 43, 61, 58, 49, 72, 58, 63, 43, 45, 72, 43

Practice 9A mark: /8

ISBN 978 1 4886 1399 9

Pearson Mathematics Homework Program 7

Statistics and probability

Skills 9B

Skills & Practice: Total marks /23

Name: ....

Class: ....

Teacher: ....

This side of this worksheet reviews number skills. The other side of this worksheet refers to *Pearson Mathematics 7* Chapter 9 'Statistics and probability' sections 9.3, 9.4 and 9.5.

1 Complete the table below:

	8	5	9	4	7	3	12	2	6
$\times 9$									

2 Complete the table below:

	54	18	81	63	27	99	9	72	36
$\div 9$									

3 Find $54\,000 \div 1000$.

4 Calculate 985×54.

5 What are the next three numbers in the sequence?

4, 11, 18, 25, …

6 What is the highest common factor of 36 and 24?

7 Find $12 \div (6 \div 3)$.

8 Calculate $\frac{3}{4} \times \frac{2}{15}$.

9 What is 124.4255 rounded to 2 decimal places?

10 Evie lost 3 of 30 maths worksheets over the year. What is this as a percentage?

11 Calculate $9.73 + 6.54$.

12 Find 1^4.

13 If $35 - v = 15$, find the value of v.

14 Simplify $2x + 5xy + y + 3x - 2xy$.

15 What is the value of angle a?

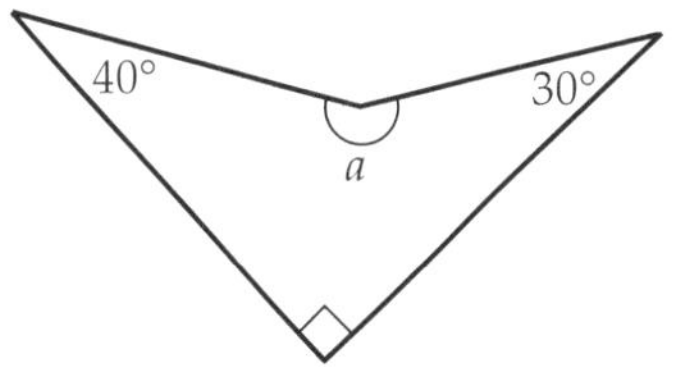

16 Find the median of these shoe sizes.
4, 7, 6, 5, 4, 3, 6

17 How many minutes are in 4 hours?

Skills 9B mark: /17

ISBN 978 1 4886 1399 9

Pearson Mathematics 7 Homework Program

Statistics and probability

Practice 9B

Show all your working

This side of this worksheet covers *Pearson Mathematics 7* Chapter 9 'Statistics and probability' sections 9.3, 9.4 and 9.5.

For online help, go to your *Pearson Mathematics 7* eBook.

1 Twelve students in a class had older siblings. Draw a dot plot to illustrate the ages of these older siblings:

17, 14, 16, 15, 16, 17, 14, 16, 15, 17, 16, 18

2 Using a class interval of 10, draw an ordered stem-and-leaf plot of the teachers' ages at a local primary school:

31, 44, 23, 28, 37, 57, 41, 25, 38, 62

3 The graph shows the average monthly rainfall (in mm) for Wetsville during the first six months of the year.

a Which is the wettest month?

b Which month has a rainfall of 28 mm?

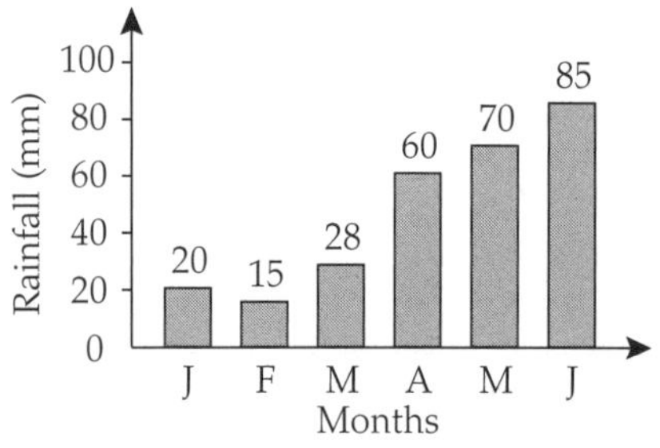

4 Sales figures for the Calculators-R-Us company over 7 years are shown below.

a What is the highest number of calculators sold?

b In which years were there fewer than 300 calculators sold?

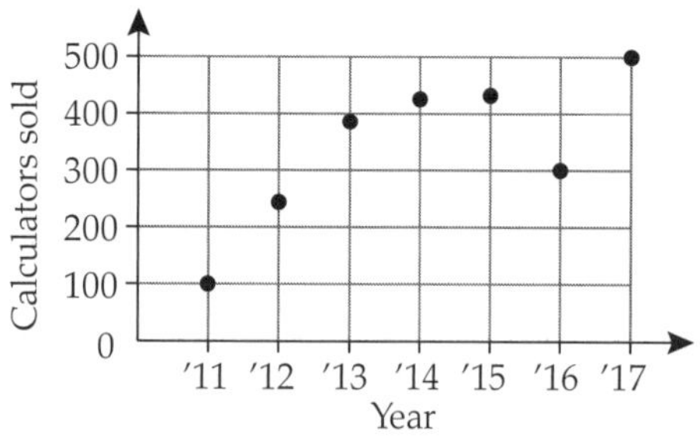

5 Draw a sector graph to represent the following data.

Pet	Number
Dog	20
Cat	14
Rat	3
Fish	1

6 Draw a divided bar graph to represent the following data.

Origin	Number
Vietnam	30
Sudan	2
Afghanistan	12
China	46

Practice 9B mark: /16

ISBN 978 1 4886 1399 9

Pearson Mathematics 7 Homework Program
Statistics and probability

Skills 9C

Skills & Practice: Total marks /27

Name:

Class:

Teacher:

This side of this worksheet reviews number skills. The other side of this worksheet refers to *Pearson Mathematics 7* Chapter 9 'Statistics and probability' sections 9.6 and 9.7.

1 Complete the table below:

	-9	5	-7	11	-4	6	-12	3	-8
+ 8									

2 Complete the table below:

	64	16	48	32	72	56	24	96	40
÷ 8									

3 Calculate 6502×100.

4 Find 957×16.

5 What are the next three numbers in the sequence?

2, 4, 7, 11, 16, …

6 Write 60 as a product of its prime factors in index form.

7 Hikers travelled from 10 m below sea level to 50 m above sea level. How many metres up have they travelled?

8 Calculate $1\frac{1}{6} - \frac{1}{3}$.

9 Insert a < or > symbol to make the statement true.

$\frac{33}{8}$ ☐ $\frac{18}{4}$

10 What is 80% of 100 km?

11 Find 0.8×0.8.

12 Evaluate $\sqrt{121}$.

13 If $16 + s = 16$, find the value of s.

14 Simplify $10a + 5a + 2b - 6a + 4b$.

15 How many sides does an octagon have?

16 Six friends go to different schools. The number of classes they have each school day are: 4, 5, 6, 6, 7, 8. What is the mean number of classes?

17 What is the area of the top of a mattress that is 2 m long and 1.8 m wide?

Skills 9C mark: /17

ISBN 978 1 4886 1399 9

Pearson Mathematics Homework Program 7

Statistics and probability

Practice 9C

Show all your working

This side of this worksheet covers *Pearson Mathematics 7* Chapter 9 'Statistics and probability' sections 9.6 and 9.7.

For online help, go to your *Pearson Mathematics 7* eBook.

1 Sienna and Sarah kept track of the number of hours of homework they did over a 5-day school week. These are their results:

Sienna: 2, 1, 2, 3, 2   Sarah: 1, 2, 3, 4, 0

Find the mean, median, mode and range for each.

2 Use your results for the previous question to compare the number of hours of homework done by Sienna and Sarah.

Monthly mean minimum temperature (°C)

	Jan	Feb	March	April	May	Jun	Jul	Aug	Sept	Oct	Nov	Dec
Broome, WA (Bidyadanga)	26.0	25.6	24.9	22.1	18.4	15.4	13.9	14.9	17.5	21.0	23.9	25.7
Adelaide, SA (Kent Town)	17.0	17.2	15.2	12.4	10.2	8.1	7.5	8.2	9.7	11.4	14.0	15.5

Source: Bureau of Meteorology

3 Calculate the various measures of centre and range for the monthly mean minimum temperatures for Broome and Adelaide given above.

4 Using your results from the previous question, compare the monthly mean minimum temperatures for these two cities.

5 Three coins are tossed at the same time in a game of 'three-up'. List all the possible combinations of results that could occur.

6 In the game of 'three-up', you win when all the coins show the same face (heads or tails). What is the probability of winning?

7 Calculate the probability of rolling an even number on a standard six-sided die.

8 Calculate the probability of picking a King from a standard pack of 52 playing cards.

9 Calculate the probability of randomly selecting a letter 'c' from the letters of the word *chocolate*.

10 Decide whether you would describe the event 'I will get homework on Monday' as 'impossible', 'not likely', 'likely' or 'certain'.

Practice 9C mark: /10

ISBN 978 1 4886 1399 9

Pearson Mathematics 7 Homework Program

Transformation and visualisation

Skills 10A

Skills & Practice: Total marks /25

Name:

Class:

Teacher:

This side of this worksheet reviews number skills. The other side of this worksheet refers to *Pearson Mathematics 7* Chapter 10 'Transformation and visualisation' sections 10.1, 10.2, 10.3 and 10.4.

1 Complete the table below:

	5	11	7	3	12	9	4	8	6
× 11									

2 Complete the table below:

	88	22	110	44	121	33	55	132	77
÷ 11									

3 Find 72 300 × 10.

4 Calculate 598 × 27.

5 What are the next three numbers in the sequence?

2, 1, 3, 2, 4, 3, 5, …

6 Find the highest common factor of 64 and 108.

7 Find 2 + -3 – 4 – -4.

8 Calculate $1\frac{3}{10} + \frac{1}{5}$.

9 Arrange these decimals in descending order.

1.001, 1.1, 1.002, 1.01, 1.0001, 1.1001

10 Find 5% of $700.

11 Find 0.27 – 0.19.

12 Find 12^2.

13 If $\frac{p}{5} = 7$, find the value of p.

14 If $x = 5$, what is the value of the expression $(x - 1) \times 3$?

15 If you are facing south and you turn 90° clockwise, which direction are you facing now?

16 What is the probability of getting 'heads' when a coin is tossed?

17 How many hours are in a week?

Skills 10A mark: /17

ISBN 978 1 4886 1399 9

Pearson Mathematics 7 Homework Program

Transformation and visualisation

Practice 10A

Show all your working

This side of this worksheet covers *Pearson Mathematics 7* Chapter 10 'Transformation and visualisation' sections 10.1, 10.2, 10.3 and 10.4.

For online help, go to your *Pearson Mathematics 7* eBook.

1 What would be the reverse translation to 3 units right and 6 units down?

2 A figure is translated 5 units left, 2 units up, 4 units right and 4 units down. What is the final position of the image compared to the original position?

3 Reflect this shape in the line *XY*.

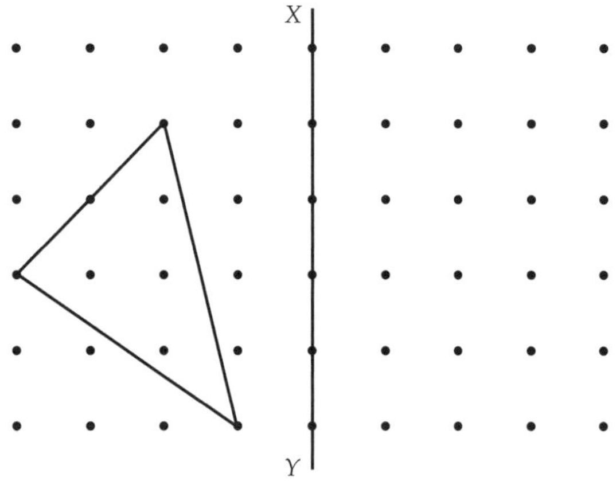

4 Rotate this shape 180° clockwise about the given point.

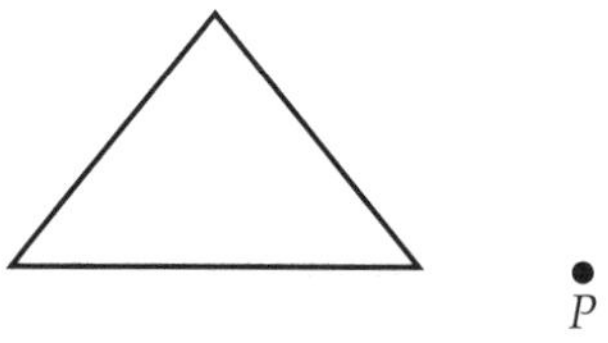

5 Draw a reflection of the following in the line of reflection shown.

6 By what minimum angle will the following shape need to be rotated so that the resulting image will match the original?

7 On the grid below, draw the image of the figure after the following transformations: rotate 90° clockwise about vertex *C* and translate 2 units down.

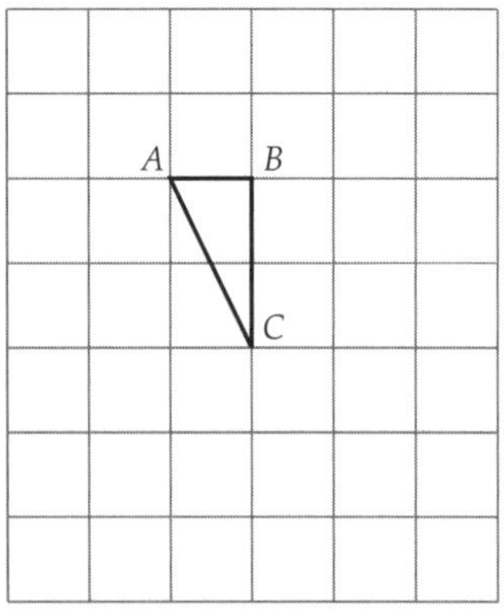

8 On the grid below, draw the image of the figure after the following transformations: Reflect along the line *BC* and translate 1 unit right.

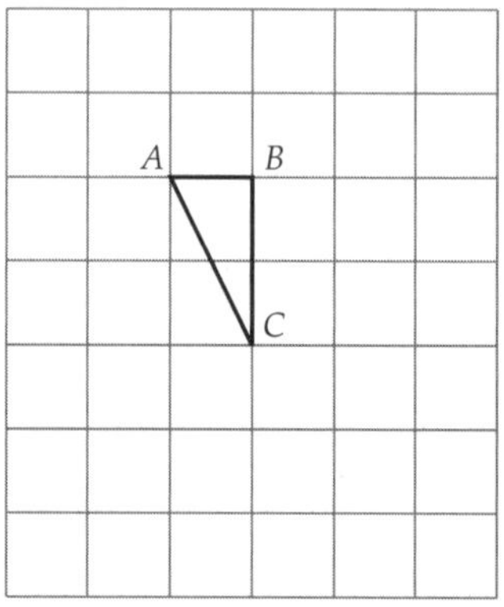

Practice 10A mark: /18

ISBN 978 1 4886 1399 9

Pearson Mathematics 7 Homework Program

Transformation and visualisation

Skills 10B

Skills & Practice: Total marks /27

Name:

Class:

Teacher:

This side of this worksheet reviews number skills. The other side of this worksheet refers to *Pearson Mathematics 7* Chapter 10 'Transformation and visualisation' sections 10.5, 10.6 and 10.7.

1 Complete the table below:

	7	4	9	6	3	11	5	12	8
× 7									

2 Complete the table below:

	56	21	63	35	14	42	84	28	49
÷ 7									

3 Evaluate 771 000 ÷ 1000.

4 Calculate 774 × 25.

5 What are the next two numbers in the sequence?

1, 5, 25, 125, …

6 Is 9 a factor of 1233?

7 Calculate (2 + -4) + (4 + -2) – (-2 – -4).

8 Find $\frac{5}{6} \times \frac{12}{15}$.

9 What is 0.499 rounded to 1 decimal place?

10 Out of 10 puppies, 3 puppies had brown fur. What is this as a percentage?

11 Find 1.23 + 3.28.

12 Calculate 3^4.

13 If $x - 12 = 12$, find the value of x.

14 Simplify $3ef + 2e + 3f - 2ef$.

15 Calculate the size of angle c.

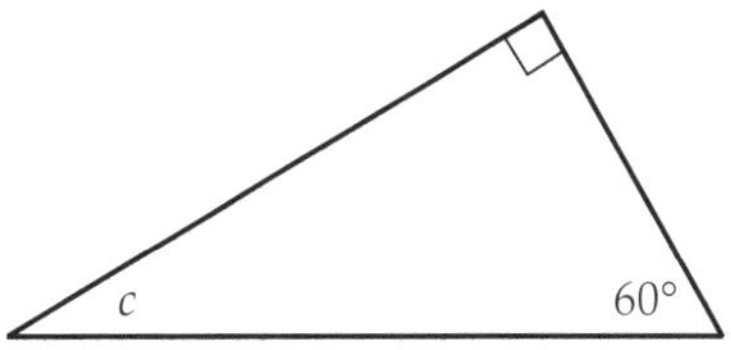

16 For one week, Reshma records how much time it takes her to walk home from school and these are her results: 12 min, 15 min, 13 min, 14 min, 11 min. What is her average time to walk home?

17 Dave is placing 16 square pavers to make a path to the back door. Each paver has a side length of 50 cm. What is the area (in cm²) of these 16 pavers altogether?

Skills 10B mark: /17

ISBN 978 1 4886 1399 9

Pearson Mathematics 7 Homework Program

Transformation and visualisation

Practice 10B

Show all your working

This side of this worksheet covers *Pearson Mathematics 7* Chapter 10 'Transformation and visualisation' sections 10.5, 10.6 and 10.7.

For online help, go to your *Pearson Mathematics 7* eBook.

1 How many lines of symmetry does an equilateral triangle have?

2 Which of the letters in the word SYMMETRY have lines of symmetry? Which of the letters in the word SYMMETRY have rotational symmetry? State their order of rotational symmetry.

3 Which of these symbols have lines of symmetry?

4 State the order of rotational symmetry of the following symbols.

5 Use the isometric dots below to draw a cube with side length of two units.

6 How many cubes would be needed to build this solid? Assume there are no holes and only two blocks between the two 'towers'.

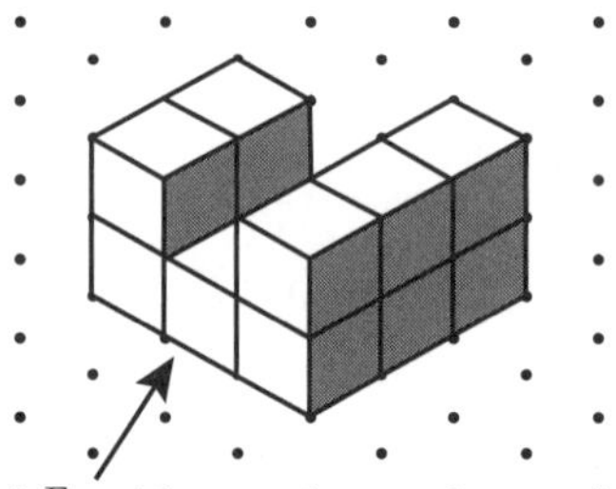

7 Draw the side view of the solid in Question 6 (i.e. the shaded side).

8 Draw the front view of the solid in Question 6.

9 Draw the top view of the solid in Question 6.

10 If the top view, side view and front view of a solid made from blocks are exactly the same, then what is the name of the solid?

Practice 10B mark: /10

  ISBN 978 1 4886 1399 9